The
BEEKMAN
1802
HEIRLOOM DESSERT
COOKBOOK

BRENT RIDGE AND JOSH KILMER-PURCELL AND SANDY GLUCK

The BEEKMAN 1802 HEIRLOOM DESSERT COOKBOOK

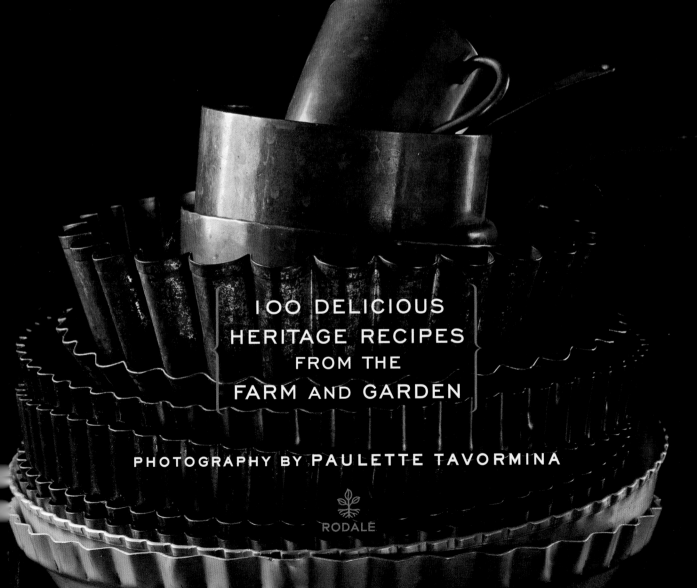

IOO DELICIOUS
HERITAGE RECIPES
FROM THE
FARM AND GARDEN

PHOTOGRAPHY BY PAULETTE TAVORMINA

RODALE

Rodale books may be purchased for business or promotional use or for special sales. For information, please write to:
Special Markets Department, Rodale Inc., 733 Third Avenue, New York, NY 10017

Printed in the United States of America
Rodale Inc. makes every effort to use acid-free ∞, recycled paper ♻.

Photographs by Paulette Tavormina
except for pages 4, 9, 49, 50, 59, 61, 62–63, 70, 75, 84, 95, 99, 126–127, 138, 158–159, 171, 176–177, 179, 186, 192–193, 202, 216–217, 218–219

Book design by Amy C. King
Food styling by Paul Grimes
Prop styling by Thom Driver

Library of Congress Cataloging-in-Publication Data is on file with the publisher.
ISBN 978-1-60961-573-4 hardcover

Distributed to the trade by Macmillan
2 4 6 8 10 9 7 5 3 1 hardcover

We inspire and enable people to improve their lives and the world around them.
RODALEBOOKS.COM

FOR GENERATIONS

Contents

INTRODUCTION

Once in a young lifetime one should be allowed to have as much sweetness as one can possibly want and hold.

—JUDITH OLNEY

Over the past two decades, dessert fads have come and gone. Doughnuts, cream puffs, rice pudding, frozen yogurt, cupcakes, macaroons, whoopie pies, and cake pops have all had recent resurrections and reincarnations.

Such popularity peaks speak not to the fickleness of the sweet tooth, but more so to the enduring place that desserts *of all types* have in our memories. What family doesn't have at least one gooey, syrupy, creamy, decadent recipe that they beg Mom to make every time they go home? The good times associated with such delights make them even sweeter and are what make certain dessert traditions enduring endpoints to our American celebrations.

WHAT MAKES AN HEIRLOOM RECIPE?

When we created the award-winning book *The Beekman 1802 Heirloom Recipe Cookbook*, we were quickly confronted with the question, "What's an heirloom recipe?"

At Beekman 1802, we believe that "heirlooms" of any type have a sentimental or intrinsic value greater than their assigned monetary figure. They are at times virtually irreplaceable, and because of this they are treasured and passed down from one generation to the next.

An heirloom recipe is one that is made so frequently or holds such special esteem in a family's culinary canon that the dish itself has developed its own mythology and its own lore.

"Aunt Hazel's oatmeal cookies were so good and sold so well at the bake sale that she practically built that new church fellowship hall herself!"

"Mamaw's banana pudding made a grown man cry—twice!"

In order for a recipe to be made so many times that it develops these complex layers of nostalgia, it must meet several criteria:

1. *IT MUST BE DELICIOUS.*
2. *IT MUST BE (RELATIVELY) SIMPLE TO MAKE.*
3. *IT MUST HAVE INGREDIENTS THAT ARE READILY AVAILABLE TO EVERYONE.*

And these are exactly the types of recipes we've included in this book—recipes that are meant to help you create memories around your table.

FOUR SEASONS OF SWEETNESS

Life at Beekman 1802 Farm revolves around the seasons, and everything that we do or create is meant to exalt what nature has already started. Certain recipes that mother made were at the direction of Mother Nature.

Grandma may have made the *best* fruitcake, but she would not have served it at the Fourth of July picnic. The hand-churned frozen custard that cools our tongue and melts our hearts in summer is not as welcome at Christmas. Our palates have a seasonality, no matter how sugar-coated the treat.

Taking classic recipes, we give each a unique Beekman twist that will surprise and please even those who believe that the way they've always made it can't be perfected.

Like any heirloom, these recipes are meant to show the patina that comes from frequent use, and we've designed special sidebars so that you can keep your own notes and make each recipe your own. They will evolve over time. With that, it becomes not *our* cookbook but *your* cookbook. A memory embedded on every page.

So prepare to laugh. Prepare to smile and swoon. Prepare to referee who gets to lick the spoon, the bowl, the beater.

The secret ingredient in every recipe in this book is not just sugar, but a magical dust that when liberally sprinkled has the power to enrapture us.

RECIPES

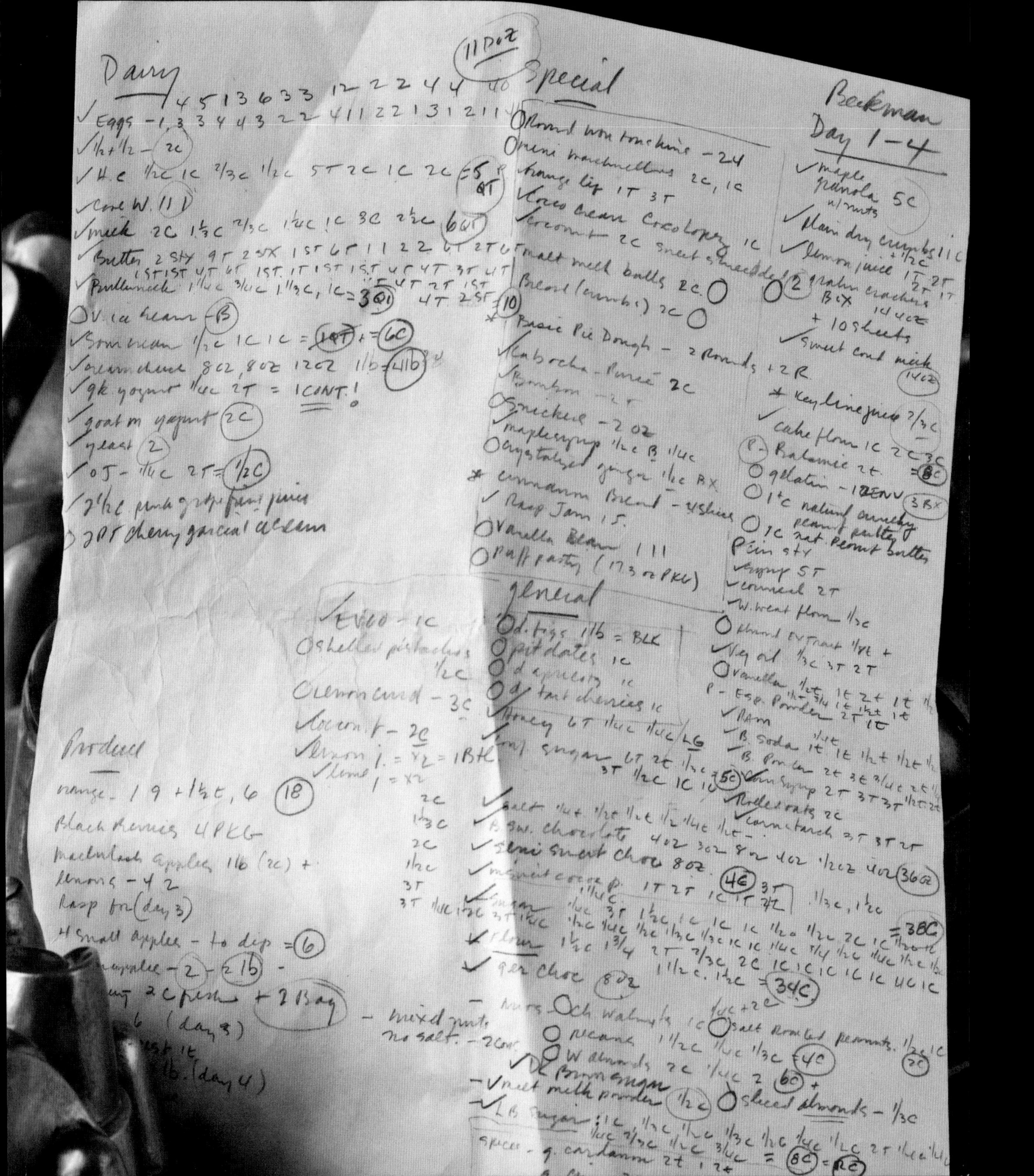

Dairy

√ Eggs — 1, 3 3 4 4 3 2 2 4 1 2 2 1 3 1 2 1 1   (11 Doz)

√ ½ + ½ — 2c

√ H.c ½c 1c ⅔c ½c 5T 2c 1c 2c = 5 QT

√ cow W. 11 T

√ milk 2c 1⅓c ⅔c 1¼c 1c 3c 2½c 6 QT

Butter 2 stx 4T 2 stx 1 st 6T 1 1 2 2 6T 2T 6T
1st 1st 4T 6T 1st 1T 1st 1st 4T 4T 3T 4T

√ Buttermilk 1¼c 3/4c 1⅓c, 1c = 3 QT   4T 2 5T (10)

○ V ice cream — (B)

√ Sour cream ½c 1c 1c = 18T + = (6c)

√ cream cheese 8 oz, 8 oz 12 oz 1 lb = 4 lb

√ gk. yogurt ¼c 2T = 1 CONT.!

○ goat m yogurt (2c)

○ yeast (2)

√ o J — ¼c 2T = ½C

○ 2½c pink grapefruit juice

○ 2 PT cherry garcial cream

Produce

orange — 1 9 + 1½c, 6 (18)

Blackberries 4 PKG

macintosh apples 1 lb (2c) +

lemons — 4 2

Rasp for (day 3)

+ small apples — to dip = (6)

○ pineapple — 2 — 2 lb —

□ 2 c fresh + 2 Bag

6 (day 3)

est it

lb. (day 4)

Special

○ Round won ton skins — 24

○ mini marshmallows 2c, 1c

○ orange lig 1T 3T

○ coco cream Cocoloopy 1c

√ coconut 2c sweet shredded

○ malt milk balls 2c ○

○ Bread (crumbs) 2c ○

‡ Basic Pie Dough — 2 Rounds + 2 R

√ Kabocha Puree 2c

√ pumpkin — 2 c

○ Snickers — 2 oz

maple syrup ½c B ¼c

○ crystalized ginger ½c BX

‡ cinnamon Bread — 4 slices

√ Rasp Jam, 5.

○ Vanilla Bean 1 1 1

○ Puff pastry (17.3 oz PKG)

General

○ EV oo — 1c

○ shelled pistachios ½c

○ lemon curd — 3c

√ corn f. — 2c

√ lemon 1. = ½ = 1 Btl

√ lime 1. = ½

○ d. figs 1 lb = BLK

○ pit dates 1c

○ d apricots 1c

○ d/tart cherries 1c

√ honey 6T ¼c ¼c LG

√ corn sugar 6T 2c ¼c 3T ½c 1c 1c

2c
1⅓c
2c
½c
3T
3T ¼c ¼c 2T ½c

√ salt ¼t ½c ¼c ½ ¼c ¼c —

√ B. sw. chocolate 4 oz 3 oz 8 oz 4 oz ½ oz 4 oz (36 oz)

√ semi sweet choc 8 oz

√ nonsweet cocoa P. 1T 2T 1c 1T 7c (4c) 3T

√ Sugar ¼c 3T 1½c 1c 1c ½c ½c 2c 1c
¼c ¼c ¼c ⅓c 1c 1c 1½c ¼c ½c = 38C

√ flour 1½c 1¾ 2T ⅔c 2c 1c 1c 1c 4c 1c
1½c ¼c = 34C

√ ger choc 8 oz

— nuts ○ch walnuts 1c
○ pecans 1½c ¼c ⅓c (4c)
√ W almonds 2c ¼c 2 (60) +
√ brown sugar
√ sweet milk powder (½c) ○ sliced almonds — ⅓c
√ L.B. sugar 1c ½c ¼c ¼c ½c ⅓c ½c ¼c ½c 2T ¼c ¼
spices — g. cardamom 2t 2 c = (8c) = (RC)

Beekman
Day 1 - 4

√ maple granola 5c w/ nuts

√ plain dry crumbs 1 1c + ½c

√ lemon juice 1½c 2T 2T 1T

○ 2 graham crackers B. 2c X 14 4 oz
+ 10 sheets

√ sweet cond milk (14 oz)

+ key lime juice ⅔c ?

√ cake flour 1c 2c 3c

P - Balsamic 2t (8c)

○ gelatin — 12 ENV (3 BX)

○ 1½c natural crunchy peanut butter
○ 1c nat peanut butter

P cin 3t

√ nutmeg 5T

√ cornmeal 2T

W. wheat flour ½c

○ almond extract ¼t +

√ veg oil ⅓c 3T 2T

○ vanilla ¼t ¼t 1t 2t 1t 1t ½
P - Esp. powder 2T 1c

√ Rum

√ B. soda ¼t ¼t 1t 1c 1½t + ½t ½
√ B. Powder 2t 3t 3/4c 2t ½
○ corn syrup 2T 3T 3T ½t 2t ¼
√ rolled oats 2c
√ cornstarch 3T 3T 2T
1½c, 1½c

○ salt roasted peanuts ½c 1c (2c)

Winter

Winter

LEMON MERINGUE PIE 7   BASIC PIE DOUGH 8

VANILLA PANNA COTTA SURPRISE 11

WINTER KABOCHA SQUASH PIE 13

CHOCOLATE ROCKY ROAD POTSTICKERS 16

CHOCOLATE-ESPRESSO SOUP WITH MARSHMALLOWS 20

LEMON CURD 22

SNOW CREAM WITH SWEETENED CONDENSED MILK 23

SALTY NOUGAT FUDGE BROWNIES 25

BLONDIES WITH WHITE CHOCOLATE AND MACADAMIAS 26

MALTED MILK CHOCOLATE CAKE 30   RICOTTA BLINTZES 31

FRUITCAKE 33   STICKY TOFFEE PUDDING BUNS 36

SUGARPLUMS 41   DOUBLE GINGER CAKE 42

MARBLE POUND CAKE 43

ORANGE-CHOCOLATE POTS DE CRÈME 45

GERMAN CHOCOLATE CAKE 47

GINGERBREAD COOKIE ICE CREAM SANDWICHES 51

FIGGY PUDDING 53   CANDIED CITRUS ZEST 55   YULE LOG 58

MUSHROOM MERINGUES 60

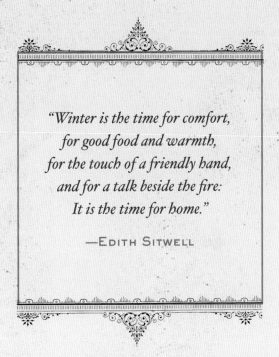

"Winter is the time for comfort,
for good food and warmth,
for the touch of a friendly hand,
and for a talk beside the fire:
It is the time for home."

—EDITH SITWELL

There is a stillness to winter on the farm that permeates the soul; the only sound for hours is the sudden pop of an ember on the fire that stirs us back to the present. Perhaps this is one of the reasons that winter holiday celebrations are so joyous and boisterous. We are awakened momentarily from our dull torpor by the glittery sites, the melody of excited voices, and a table laden with heirlooms of every variety.

LEMON MERINGUE PIE

This is the dessert Sandy's mom always made when her friend May made her annual winter visit. There's no better way to use the abundance of citrus fruits on the market shelves this time of year. It's more lemony than most, a treat for all the lemon lovers out there, and the perfect way to bring a little sunshine into a winter day.

Basic Pie Dough (page 8)

FILLING

1 cup sugar

1/3 cup cornstarch

1/4 teaspoon salt

1 cup water

3/4 cup plus 2 tablespoons fresh
    lemon juice

1/4 cup heavy cream

3 large egg yolks

MERINGUE

4 large egg whites

Pinch of salt

1/2 teaspoon cream of tartar

1/2 cup sugar

1/2 teaspoon pure vanilla extract

To make the crust: On a lightly floured work surface, roll out the dough to a 12-inch round. Roll the dough around the rolling pin and then fit it into a 9-inch pie plate without stretching it, pressing the dough into the bottom and against the sides of the pan. With a pair of scissors or a paring knife, trim the dough to leave a 1-inch overhang around the edge. Fold the overhang in over the rim to make a double layer of dough and, with your fingers, crimp the dough all around. Refrigerate for at least 1 hour before baking. (This helps to relax the dough and prevents it from shrinking once baked.)

To make the filling: Set a fine-mesh sieve over a bowl and keep at the ready for straining the filling. In a large, heavy-bottom saucepan, whisk together the sugar, cornstarch, salt, water, lemon juice, cream, and egg yolks. Cook over medium-low heat, stirring constantly, for 10 minutes, or until the mixture has the consistency of honey. Strain and let cool to room temperature.

Preheat the oven to 375°F. Line the pie shell with foil or parchment paper, leaving an overhang, and fill with pie weights or dried beans to weight the crust down. Bake for 30 minutes, then remove the foil (or paper) and weights and bake 10 minutes longer, or until baked through and crisp. Increase the oven temperature to 450°F.

To make the meringue: In a bowl, with an electric mixer, beat the egg whites and salt until foamy. Add the cream of tartar and beat until soft peaks form. Gradually, about 1 tablespoon at a time, add the sugar, beating until stiff, glossy peaks form, adding in the vanilla toward the end. Scoop the meringue onto the filling, making sure it covers the filling completely and is anchored to the crust. Use a spatula to make large swoops in the meringue. Bake for 5 minutes, or until the meringue is set and browned in spots. Let cool. Serve at room temperature or chilled.

Notes

BASIC PIE DOUGH

Josh has perfected his piecrust. This pie dough is enough for one pie but can easily be doubled for a double-crust pie. If you can find good lard at a local butcher, you can sub in 4 tablespoons of lard for 4 tablespoons of the butter; chill the lard before using. The secret to flaky piecrust is keeping the butter ice cold right up to the point that the dough goes into the oven.

1¼ cups all-purpose flour
(spooned into cup and
leveled off)

1 tablespoon sugar

¼ teaspoon salt

8 tablespoons (1 stick) cold
unsalted butter, cut into bits

3 to 4 tablespoons ice water

In a large bowl, whisk together the flour, sugar, and salt. Add the butter and with a pastry blender or 2 knives used scissor-fashion, cut in the butter until large pea-size bits are formed. Add just enough of the ice water so the mixture holds together when pinched between 2 fingers. Shape into a disk, wrap in waxed paper or plastic wrap, and refrigerate for at least 1 hour or up to 2 days. (The dough can also be well wrapped and frozen up to 3 months.)

TIP: *If you prefer, you can easily make the dough in a food processor. Pulse the flour, sugar, and salt together. Next, add the butter and pulse 10 times or until large pea-size bits are formed. With the motor running, gradually add the ice water until the dough begins to come together but doesn't form a ball. Follow the directions above for chilling.*

Notes

VANILLA PANNA COTTA SURPRISE

Some desserts reach "heirloom" status because of how they taste, others because of how they visually surprise. This wonderful Italian dessert, panna cotta—it translates to "cooked cream" but is really so much more than that—is cool, light, and refreshing. Essentially an egg-less pudding, it's the perfect ending to any meal. Ours has more milk than cream, and tucked inside is a surprise spoonful of lemon curd. When you dig into it with your spoon, it looks like you've cut open a hard-cooked egg. While too much gelatin can make things rubbery, this panna cotta turns out of its mold easily while remaining slightly jiggly.

½ cup Lemon Curd (page 22)

1 envelope (¼ ounce) plain
    unflavored gelatin

2 cups milk

1 cup heavy cream

½ cup sugar

Pinch of salt

1 vanilla bean, split lengthwise

Make the Lemon Curd and chill.

In a glass measuring cup, sprinkle the gelatin over 1 cup of the milk and let stand for about 5 minutes, or until softened.

Meanwhile, in a small saucepan, combine the remaining 1 cup milk, the cream, sugar, and salt. Scrape the vanilla seeds into the pan and add the vanilla bean. Bring to a gentle simmer over medium-low heat.

Add the softened gelatin, stirring until dissolved. Remove the vanilla bean and rinse, dry, and reserve it for another use. Pour half of the mixture into eight 6-ounce ramekins or custard cups. Refrigerate for 45 minutes to 1 hour, or until the mixture starts to set up.

Spoon 1 tablespoon of Lemon Curd over the panna cotta in the rame-kins, gently spreading it almost to the edge of the dish. Pour the remaining panna cotta mixture over the tops and refrigerate for at least 4 hours, or until set.

To serve, run a small metal spatula around the edge of the panna cotta and invert onto serving plates.

Notes

WINTER KABOCHA SQUASH PIE

f you love pumpkin pie, then you'll also love this dessert (most canned "pumpkin" on the grocery store shelf is actually winter squash). Kabocha is a type of winter squash (like pumpkin, butternut, acorn, and others) with deep orange flesh and a somewhat dry texture reminiscent of chestnuts. It is sweet and delicious.

Basic Pie Dough (page 8)

2 cups kabocha squash puree

½ cup granulated sugar

½ cup packed light brown sugar

⅔ cup heavy cream

⅔ cup milk

2 large eggs

2 tablespoons bourbon or Scotch

2 tablespoons all-purpose flour

1 teaspoon ground cinnamon

1 teaspoon ground ginger

¼ teaspoon ground cloves

TIP: *You'll need about 2 pounds of large (unpeeled) squash chunks to get 2 cups of puree. Roast them in a pan covered with foil in a 400°F oven until soft. Then scrape the flesh off the skin and puree in a food processor.*

On a lightly floured work surface, roll out the dough to a 12-inch round. Roll the dough around the rolling pin and then fit it into a 9-inch pie plate without stretching it, pressing the dough into the bottom and against the sides of the pan. With a pair of scissors or a paring knife, trim the dough to leave a 1-inch overhang around the edge. Fold the overhang in over the rim to make a double layer of dough and, with your fingers, crimp the dough all around. Refrigerate for at least 1 hour before baking (this helps to relax the dough and prevents it from shrinking once baked).

Preheat the oven to 350°F.

In a large bowl, whisk together the kabocha puree, the granulated and brown sugars, cream, milk, eggs, and bourbon. Stir in the flour, cinnamon, ginger, and cloves.

Pour the mixture into the pie shell and bake for 45 minutes, or until the pie is set with a slightly wobbly center. Cool on a wire rack. Serve at room temperature or chilled.

Notes

CHOCOLATE ROCKY ROAD POTSTICKERS

hether it be your collection of vintage ornaments or a sparkly new sweater, holiday parties are a time to show off. This clever riff on rocky road ice cream—chocolate, nuts, and marshmallows—rises to the challenge. These dumplings will also be a new and welcome addition to the parade of traditional Christmas cookies, an heirloom recipe in the making! If you'd like, you can replace a tablespoon or two of the vegetable oil with toasted sesame oil for a slightly nutty flavor.

24 round wonton skins

4 ounces bittersweet chocolate (60% cacao), finely chopped or grated

1 cup finely chopped walnuts

72 mini marshmallows

1 large egg, lightly beaten

⅓ cup vegetable oil

1 tablespoon unsweetened cocoa powder

2 teaspoons confectioners' sugar

Working with 3 wonton skins at a time (and keeping the remainder either under a dampened paper towel or plastic wrap), place 1 teaspoon chocolate, about ½ teaspoon walnuts, and 3 mini marshmallows in the center of each wonton skin, leaving a ⅓-inch border all around. Brush the bottom edge with the beaten egg. Fold the top half over and press to seal. Repeat with the remaining wonton skins, chocolate, walnuts, and marshmallows. (At this point, the potstickers can be placed in a container and frozen for up to 3 months.)

Heat half the oil in a large nonstick skillet over medium-low heat. Add 6 potstickers at a time and cook for 1½ minutes per side, or until golden brown and crisp. Remove with a slotted spoon or spatula to paper towels to drain. After half the potstickers are cooked, add the remaining oil to the pan and cook the remaining potstickers.

In a small bowl, stir together the cocoa powder and confectioners' sugar. Dust the potstickers with the mixture and serve warm.

TIP: *Wonton skins can be found either in the produce section or the freezer section of most supermarkets. They come in packages of about 50, so once you're done with what you need, freeze (or refreeze) the remainder.*

Notes

CHOCOLATE-ESPRESSO SOUP WITH MARSHMALLOWS

SERVES 4

or chocolate lovers, hot chocolate is a winter rite of passage. We wanted to elevate this cup of goodness to full-blown dessert status. Our chocolate soup is thicker than hot chocolate and thinner than pudding. If you're not a fan of coffee, simply leave it out. For the adults, if you're so inclined, add a splash of dark rum or orange liqueur at serving time.

2 cups milk

½ cup heavy cream

3 tablespoons sugar

2 tablespoons espresso powder

¼ teaspoon salt

8 ounces bittersweet chocolate, coarsely chopped

1⅓ cups mini marshmallows, or more to taste

In a medium, heavy-bottom saucepan, bring the milk, cream, sugar, espresso powder, and salt to a gentle simmer over low heat.

Whisk in the chocolate and cook, whisking constantly, until the chocolate has melted and the mixture is smooth. Ladle into warmed shallow bowls. Divide the marshmallows among the bowls and serve hot.

Notes _____

_____

_____

LEMON CURD

Lemon curd—silky smooth, the best lemon pudding you've ever had—is great as a tart filling, as part of another dessert (see Coconut Cake, page 77, and Vanilla Panna Cotta Surprise, page 11), or just on its own. To serve the lemon curd as a dessert, fold 1 cup whipped cream into it and spoon into dessert dishes. Top it with berries or more whipped cream.

3 large eggs

3 large egg yolks

½ cup fresh lemon juice

½ cup sugar

8 tablespoons (1 stick) unsalted
    butter, cut into bits

Set a fine-mesh sieve over a bowl and keep at the ready for straining the curd. In a double boiler or a large bowl set over, not in, a pan of simmering water, whisk together the whole eggs, egg yolks, lemon juice, sugar, and butter. Cook over low heat, whisking constantly, for 5 minutes, or until the mixture has the consistency of honey. Strain into the bowl.

Place a sheet of plastic wrap directly on the curd and let cool to room temperature. (You can transfer the curd to a jar, cover, and refrigerate for up to 3 weeks.)

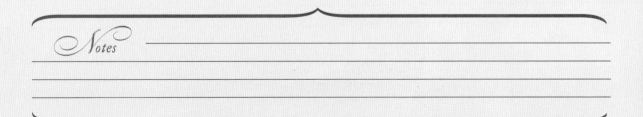

Notes

SNOW CREAM WITH SWEETENED CONDENSED MILK

*B*rent used to think his grandma had magical powers when she created sweet ice cream out of snow. On the farm, when winter arrives, we've got lots of clean fresh snow to use for snow cream. Straight up it's delicious, but for variety you could drizzle some Fudge Topping (page 179) or a little coffee liqueur over the top.

1 can (14 ounces) sweetened
   condensed milk

2 teaspoons pure vanilla extract

1 teaspoon grated lemon zest

2 teaspoons fresh lemon juice

8 cups snow or shaved ice

In a bowl, whisk together the condensed milk, vanilla, lemon zest, and lemon juice.

Place the snow or shaved ice in a bowl, pour the condensed milk mixture over it, and with a fork mix quickly to combine.

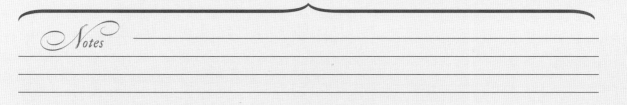

Notes

SALTY NOUGAT FUDGE BROWNIES

There are nearly as many brownie recipes as there are moms. While research (our own) has shown that there's rarely ever a bad brownie recipe, we couldn't resist adding our own twist. Roasted peanuts with a little salt and a Snickers bar all packed in a rich brownie? Not too shabby! If you like, you can wrap each brownie individually and freeze for up to 3 months.

Softened butter for the pan

4 ounces bittersweet chocolate, coarsely chopped

6 tablespoons (¾ stick) unsalted butter

2 large eggs

½ cup granulated sugar

⅓ cup packed light brown sugar

2 tablespoons light corn syrup

1 teaspoon pure vanilla extract

¼ teaspoon salt

⅔ cup all-purpose flour (spooned into cup and leveled off)

½ cup salted roasted peanuts, coarsely chopped

1 Snickers bar (1.83 ounces), coarsely chopped

Preheat the oven to 350°F. Butter an 8 × 8-inch baking pan. Line the bottom with parchment paper, leaving a 2-inch overhang on two sides. Butter the paper lining the bottom.

In a heatproof bowl set over, not in, a pan of simmering water, combine the chocolate and butter and stir to melt.

In a large bowl, whisk together the eggs, granulated and brown sugars, corn syrup, vanilla, and salt until combined. Stir in the chocolate mixture and the flour. Fold in the nuts and the candy bar. Scrape the batter into the pan.

Bake for 40 minutes, or until set around the edges and a wooden pick inserted in the center comes out with some moist crumbs attached. Let cool in the pan.

To serve, use the overhang to lift the cooled sheet of brownies from the pan, then cut into 12 serving pieces.

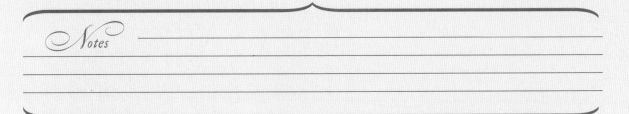

Notes

BLONDIES WITH WHITE CHOCOLATE AND MACADAMIAS

ires in the fireplace and family gatherings each bring their own kind of warmth. Winter seems tailor-made for comfort foods. While we always preferred brownies, a few extra sparks to the traditional blondie recipe have helped us see the light. Dark brown sugar has mellow molasses notes that combine with rich macadamia nuts and white chocolate to make these blondies special.

Softened butter and flour for the pan

8 tablespoons (1 stick) unsalted butter, at room temperature

¾ cup packed dark brown sugar

1 large egg

1 teaspoon pure vanilla extract

1 cup all-purpose flour (spooned into cup and leveled off)

½ teaspoon baking soda

½ teaspoon salt

½ cup macadamia nuts, coarsely chopped

½ cup coarsely chopped white chocolate or white chocolate chips

Preheat the oven to 350°F. Butter and flour an 8 × 8-inch baking pan. Line the bottom of the pan with parchment paper, leaving a 2-inch overhang on two sides. Butter and flour the paper lining the bottom.

In a small skillet, melt the butter over medium heat. Cook for 2 minutes, or until the butter gets foamy, the foam subsides, and the butter is browned in spots. Immediately remove from the heat, transfer to a bowl, and whisk in the brown sugar. Whisk in the egg and vanilla.

Stir in the flour, baking soda, and salt. Fold in the nuts and white chocolate and scrape the batter into the pan.

Bake for 25 minutes, or until set around the edges and a wooden pick inserted in the center comes out with some moist crumbs attached. Let cool in the pan.

To serve, use the overhang to lift the cooled sheet of blondies from the pan, then cut into 12 serving pieces.

TIP: *When you brown the butter, be sure to use a skillet with a light-colored interior so you can monitor the color of the butter.*

Notes

MALTED MILK CHOCOLATE CAKE

Somewhere in Wisconsin, Josh developed an affinity for old-fashioned soda shops. Lime rickeys, egg creams, and root beer floats all have a special place in his heart that even a wintery cold snap can't melt. Malteds are a popular soda fountain drink, and chocolate cake is an all-time favorite dessert; here they pair up for an unexpected double malted flavor that's as sweet as lips bumping together over a straw. Malted milk powder is available in the supermarket alongside the cocoa.

Softened butter and flour for
    the pan

½ cup malted milk powder

1⅓ cups milk

1½ teaspoons pure vanilla extract

1¾ cups all-purpose flour
    (spooned into cup and
    leveled off)

1 cup unsweetened cocoa
    powder

2 teaspoons baking powder

1 teaspoon baking soda

½ teaspoon salt

8 ounces (2 sticks) unsalted
    butter, at room temperature

1 cup granulated sugar

1 cup packed light brown sugar

4 large eggs, at room
    temperature

1 cup coarsely chopped malted
    milk balls

Preheat the oven to 350°F. Butter a 9 × 13-inch baking pan. Line the bottom with parchment or waxed paper. Butter and flour the paper.

In a bowl, dissolve the malted milk powder in the milk. Stir in the vanilla. In a separate bowl, whisk together the flour, cocoa powder, baking powder, baking soda, and salt.

In a bowl, with an electric mixer on medium speed, beat together the butter and granulated and brown sugars until fluffy. Beat in the eggs, one at a time, beating well after each addition. With the mixer on low speed, alternately add the flour mixture and the milk mixture, beginning and ending with the flour mixture. Scrape the batter into the pan. Scatter the malted milk balls over the top.

Bake for 40 minutes, or until a wooden pick inserted in the center comes out clean with some moist crumbs attached and the sides of the cake start to pull away from the pan.

Transfer to a wire rack to cool and serve the cake from the pan.

Notes

RICOTTA BLINTZES

What's a blintz? It's a delicious egg-based crepe, traditional in Eastern European kitchens that can be filled with anything from farmer cheese to cooked fruit or potato. You can make these a day ahead and keep them refrigerated, or you can freeze them; just thaw before filling. You'll be amazed at all of the sweet things you discover you can roll up inside.

CREPES

¾ cup milk

¾ cup all-purpose flour
    (spooned into cup and
    leveled off)

2 tablespoons sugar

⅛ teaspoon salt

2 large eggs

2 tablespoons unsalted butter,
    plus more for the skillet,
    melted

FILLING

1 container (15 ounces) ricotta
    cheese

1 large egg

¼ cup packed light brown sugar

1¼ teaspoons pure vanilla extract

¼ teaspoon ground cinnamon

½ cup orange marmalade or
    apricot jam

Butter for the baking dish

Confectioners' sugar (optional)

To make the crepes: In a blender, combine the milk, flour, sugar, salt, eggs, and melted butter and blend until smooth. Refrigerate for at least 1 hour.

Brush a small skillet with some melted butter and heat over medium-low heat. Add about 3 tablespoons of batter to the pan and swirl the pan to evenly coat the bottom. Cook for 30 seconds, or until set and lightly browned on the underside. Lift the crepe either with a small spatula or your fingers and flip it over. Cook 10 seconds longer, then turn it out onto a plate. Repeat with the remaining batter to make 12 crepes, stacking the crepes.

Preheat the oven to 350°F.

To make the filling: In a food processor, process the ricotta until smooth, about 1 minute. Add the egg, brown sugar, vanilla, and cinnamon and pulse to combine.

Lay the crepes on a work surface and spread each with 2 teaspoons of the marmalade. Divide the filling among them, spooning it onto the bottom half of each and leaving a 1-inch border on the bottom and the sides. Fold the sides in over the filling, then roll up from the bottom to enclose. Butter a 7 × 11-inch or 9 × 9-inch baking dish (or a baking dish large enough to hold the blintzes in a single layer). Arrange the blintzes in the dish.

Bake for 10 minutes, or until lightly crisped. Serve each person 2 blintzes, sprinkled with confectioners' sugar, if desired.

Notes

FRUITCAKE

If you think of fruitcake as something leaden, better to be used as a doorstop, think again. This fruitcake, based on a Caribbean black fruitcake (which gets its dark color from burnt sugar, though we've replaced that here with molasses), is tender, not overly sweet, and packed full of fruit. Choose dark flavored fruit, such as prunes, dates, or currants; and brighter ones, such as cherries and pineapple. Then punctuate the flavors with some candied citron, orange, or lemon peel. Use whatever combo of dried fruit you like as long as it adds up to 2¼ pounds.

¾ pound pitted prunes

4 ounces dried currants

3 ounces golden raisins

4 ounces dried apricots

3 ounces candied orange peel

3 ounces candied citron

3 ounces candied pineapple

4 ounces dried cherries

2 cups sweet red wine or
  grape juice

1 cup dark rum

Softened butter for the pan

1 cup natural (skin-on) almonds

3 cups all-purpose flour
  (spooned into cup and
  leveled off)

2 teaspoons baking soda

1 teaspoon ground allspice

1 teaspoon ground cinnamon

1 teaspoon freshly grated
  nutmeg

½ teaspoon salt

8 ounces (2 sticks) unsalted
  butter, at room temperature

1⅓ cups packed dark brown sugar

5 large eggs, at room
  temperature

½ cup molasses (not blackstrap)

2 teaspoons pure vanilla extract

In a large plastic or glass container with a cover, combine the prunes, currants, raisins, apricots, orange peel, citron, pineapple, and cherries. Add 1½ cups of the sweet wine and the rum, cover, and let stand at room temperature for at least 2 days or up to 3 weeks, shaking the container twice a day.

Preheat the oven to 300°F. Generously butter three 8 × 4-inch loaf pans.

Working in batches, puree the fruit and the soaking liquid with the almonds in a food processor, pulsing until coarsely ground.

In a large bowl, whisk together the flour, baking soda, allspice, cinnamon, nutmeg, and salt.

In a bowl, with an electric mixer on medium speed, beat the butter and brown sugar until well combined. Add the eggs, one at a time, beating well after each addition. Beat in the molasses and vanilla. Gradually beat in the flour mixture, then stir in the fruit mixture.

Scrape the batter into the pans and cover with foil. Bake for 1 hour 50 minutes, or until a wooden pick inserted in the center of a cake comes out clean. Cool in the pans on a wire rack, then run a small metal spatula around the sides of the cakes and invert (right side up) onto the rack to cool completely.

Sprinkle the tops of the cakes with the remaining ½ cup wine, then double-wrap the cakes in parchment paper and foil. They can be served immediately or stored in a cool, dry place for up to a month.

Notes _____

_____

_____

_____

STICKY TOFFEE PUDDING BUNS

One of the first "fancy" dining experiences we ever had was at a restaurant in New York City called Aureole. Despite the delicious and beautiful cuisine, what made it most fancy for us was at the end of the meal we were given a beautiful bag with a pastry to enjoy for breakfast the next morning. It had an impact on us, and we try to put this level of thought and care into every Beekman 1802 experience that people have—whether it's using one of our products or coming to one of our many festivals in Sharon Springs, New York. When we have dinner guests at the farm who aren't spending the night, we always send them home with a goodie bag. A pleasant memory the following morning is the best part of any meal.

BUNS

1 envelope (¼ ounce,
    2½ teaspoons) active
    dry yeast

½ cup warm milk (105° to 110°F)

2 cups all-purpose flour
    (spooned into cup and
    leveled off), plus more
    for rolling

3 tablespoons sugar

½ teaspoon salt

2 large egg yolks

6 tablespoons (¾ stick) unsalted
    butter, melted

Vegetable oil for the bowl

FILLING

8 ounces dates, pitted

⅓ cup orange or tangerine juice

To make the buns: In a small bowl, sprinkle the yeast over the milk and let stand for 5 minutes, or until foamy.

In a food processor, combine the flour, sugar, and salt and pulse to combine. With the machine running, add the egg yolks, butter, and yeast mixture and process for 1 minute. Transfer the dough to an oiled bowl, turning the dough to coat. Cover with plastic wrap and let rise until doubled in bulk, 1½ to 2 hours.

To make the filling: Meanwhile, boil a large pot of water over high heat. Place the dates in a small heatproof bowl and add boiling water to cover. Let stand for 5 to 10 minutes, or until very soft. Drain and chop the dates. Place the dates in a bowl with the orange juice and mix well to combine.

To make the topping: Pour 6 tablespoons of the butter into a 9 × 13-inch baking pan. Sprinkle with the brown sugar.

Punch the dough down. On a lightly floured surface, with your hands or a rolling pin, pat or roll the dough out to a 12 × 16-inch rectangle. Brush the remaining 2 tablespoons butter over the dough and gently spread the date mixture over it, leaving a 2-inch border all around.

(continued)

Notes

TOPPING

8 tablespoons (1 stick) unsalted
  butter, melted

¾ cup packed light brown sugar

> **TIP:** *Sometimes it's hard to tell when dough has risen enough, but if you let the dough rise in an 8-cup (or larger) clear measuring cup, you can easily tell once the dough has doubled. Or, in lieu of that, press your finger into the dough; if it leaves an indentation that doesn't pop right back at you, the dough is ready.*

Starting at one short end, roll the dough into a compact cylinder. Cut crosswise into 12 equal pieces. Place in the baking pan in 4 rows of 3, leaving space between each row. Cover with plastic wrap and let rise for 1 hour, or until puffy and doubled in bulk.

Preheat the oven to 350°F. Uncover the pan and bake for 25 minutes, or until the buns are golden brown. Immediately invert onto a serving platter. Serve warm or at room temperature.

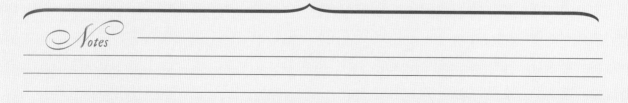

Notes

SUGARPLUMS

Most of us have heard of the sugarplum fairies, but few have actually tried the holiday delicacy that inspired the Tchaikovsky fantasy. These can be made with any combo of dried fruits and nuts (although we especially like the crisp almonds paired with the deeply flavored dates, bright apricots, and cherries). No need to roll them all at once; you can keep the mixture tightly covered in the fridge for several weeks and shape the sugarplums when needed. A perfect holiday gift or stocking stuffer when beautifully packaged.

¾ cup almonds

½ cup pitted dates

½ cup dried apricots

½ cup dried tart cherries

3 tablespoons honey

3 tablespoons confectioners' sugar, plus more for coating

¾ teaspoon ground cardamom

¾ teaspoon ground cinnamon

Pinch of salt

Preheat the oven to 350°F. Place the almonds on a rimmed baking sheet and toast for 10 minutes, or until crisp and fragrant. Let cool to room temperature.

Transfer the almonds to a food processor and add the dates, apricots, and cherries and process until the fruit and nuts are finely chopped but have not formed a ball.

Add the honey, confectioners' sugar, cardamom, cinnamon, and salt, and pulse just to combine.

With dampened hands, shape into walnut-size balls (about a rounded teaspoon each). If serving right away, roll in confectioners' sugar. If not, refrigerate between layers of waxed paper and roll in confectioners' sugar just before serving.

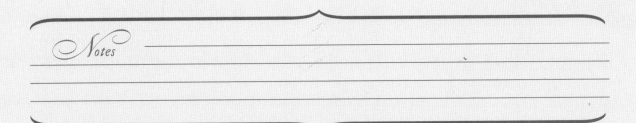

Notes

DOUBLE GINGER CAKE

W̶hen making gingerbread cookies, we always like to cut them thick (up to ¼ inch) and pull them out of the oven when the edges are crisp but the centers are still soft and moist. Our gingerbread men sired this cake recipe. Both ground and fresh ginger make this cake warm, spicy, inviting, and a perfect end to a hearty winter meal (and the perfect start to a winter morning the next day). Regular molasses, sometimes labeled "original," is what you should use here—blackstrap molasses is too strong and overpowering. If you're in the South and are so inclined, swap in sorghum for the molasses.

CAKE

Softened butter for the pan

Fine dried bread crumbs for
    the pan

Cooking spray

2½ cups all-purpose flour
    (spooned into cup and
    leveled off)

2 teaspoons baking powder

¾ teaspoon baking soda

1½ teaspoons ground ginger

1 teaspoon ground cinnamon

½ teaspoon salt

1 cup granulated sugar

¾ cup molasses (not blackstrap)

2 large eggs

12 tablespoons (1½ sticks)
    unsalted butter, melted

⅔ cup hot water

4 ounces fresh ginger, peeled
    and grated or very finely
    chopped

DRIZZLE

⅓ cup confectioners' sugar

2½ teaspoons fresh lemon juice

To make the cake: Preheat the oven to 350°F. Generously butter a 10- to 12-cup Bundt pan. Dust the pan with the bread crumbs. Coat with cooking spray.

In a large bowl, whisk together the flour, baking powder, baking soda, ground ginger, cinnamon, and salt.

In a separate bowl, whisk together the granulated sugar, molasses, eggs, butter, and hot water until smooth and well combined. Stir in the fresh ginger. Fold in the flour mixture and scrape the batter into the prepared pan.

Bake for 45 minutes, or until a wooden pick inserted in the cake comes out clean. Let cool in the pan. Run a metal spatula around the sides and center tube of the pan and invert the cake onto a cake plate.

To make the drizzle: In a small bowl, stir together the confectioners' sugar and lemon juice and drizzle over the cake.

Notes

MARBLE POUND CAKE

Oddly, the reason that we think of this as a winter dessert is that Brent's mom would send him care packages when he was away at school. Pound cake is easy to ship and to store, and Brent would often keep it in the freezer and cut off frozen slices to eat whenever the late-night sweet tooth struck. Sour cream makes this pound cake especially moist. The small amount of lemon zest gives the vanilla batter a lift. This is a perfect recipe to use when you need to send someone far away a little piece of home. (They don't have to eat it frozen!)

Softened butter for the pan

Fine dried bread crumbs for the pan

Cooking spray

2 cups all-purpose flour (spooned into cup and leveled off)

1½ teaspoons baking powder

½ teaspoon baking soda

½ teaspoon salt

8 tablespoons (1 stick) unsalted butter, at room temperature

1¼ cups sugar

4 large eggs

1 teaspoon pure vanilla extract

1 teaspoon grated lemon zest

¾ cup sour cream

4 ounces bittersweet chocolate, melted

2 tablespoons bourbon

Preheat the oven to 325°F. Generously butter a 10-cup tube pan. Dust the pan with the bread crumbs. Coat with cooking spray.

In a large bowl, whisk together the flour, baking powder, baking soda, and salt.

In a bowl, with an electric mixer on medium speed, beat the butter and sugar until light and fluffy. Add in the eggs, one at a time, beating well after each addition. Mix in the vanilla, lemon zest, and sour cream. Gradually beat in the flour mixture.

In a small bowl, stir together the chocolate, bourbon, and 1½ cups of the batter. Scrape the vanilla batter into the prepared pan, then dollop the chocolate batter on top. With a knife or a chopstick, swirl the chocolate batter through the vanilla batter.

Bake for 55 minutes to 1 hour, or until the cake starts to pull away from the sides of the pan and a wooden pick inserted in the cake comes out clean with some moist crumbs attached.

Let cool in the pan on a wire rack for 30 minutes. Run a metal spatula around the sides and center tube of the pan to loosen the cake and invert it (right side up) onto the rack to cool completely.

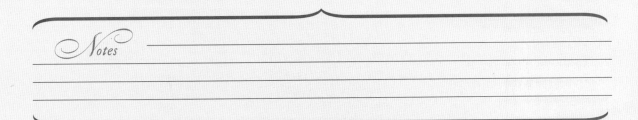

Notes

ORANGE-CHOCOLATE POTS DE CRÈME

*N*ot all of our heirloom desserts have origins as far back as our youth. Some we picked up when we started our life together. We both had our first taste of pots de crème in a restaurant on the very tip of St. Tropez. With the sea surrounding our candlelit table, two small apothecary jars were delivered. To our young and inexperienced selves, they looked like two jewels sent to cap a romantic meal. More often than not, this is the dessert we make for each other when having a Valentine's meal at home.

1⅓ cups half-and-half

Grated zest of 1 orange

Pinch of salt

¼ cup sugar

3 ounces bittersweet chocolate, coarsely chopped

3 large egg yolks

2 tablespoons unsweetened cocoa powder

1 tablespoon orange liqueur

½ teaspoon pure vanilla extract

TIP: *If you've got espresso cups or even a beautiful set of small jars, use them— it's a fun way of serving pots de crème. If you like, top each with a spoonful of whipped cream.*

Preheat the oven to 325°F.

In a small saucepan, combine the half-and-half, orange zest, and salt and bring to a simmer over low heat. Remove from the heat, cover, and let steep 15 minutes.

Strain the orange zest out of the mixture, return the half-and-half to the pan, and add the sugar. Bring to a simmer, remove from the heat, and add the chocolate. Cover and let stand for 5 minutes, or until the chocolate has melted.

In a large glass measuring cup with a spout (this makes for easier pouring), stir together the egg yolks, cocoa powder, orange liqueur, and vanilla until smooth. Stir in the chocolate mixture. (Don't beat vigorously as you don't want to create bubbles.)

Pour the custard into six 6-ounce ramekins or custard cups. Place a folded kitchen towel in the bottom of a baking pan large enough to hold the ramekins snugly. Place the ramekins in the pan and fill the pan with hot water, to come halfway up the sides of the cups. Cover the pan with foil.

Bake for 25 to 30 minutes, or until the custards are just set but slightly wobbly in the center. Uncover and carefully remove the cups from the water bath. Let cool to room temperature, then refrigerate until chilled.

Notes

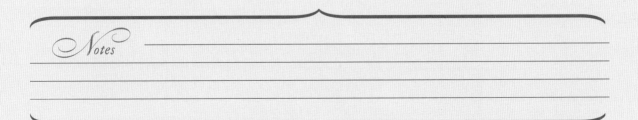

GERMAN CHOCOLATE CAKE

No, it's not chocolate from Germany, it's a brand of sweet chocolate called German's, named after Samuel German, an employee at Walter Baker & Company, who formulated the bittersweet blend. The cake was created in the 1950s and has been a favorite ever since. If you've got a sweet tooth, the combo of chocolate cake and a somewhat gooey, creamy frosting will be right up your alley. We've used some sweetened cream of coconut (think Coco Lopez—what you'd use for piña coladas) and heavy cream for the frosting base.

CAKE

Cooking spray

3 large eggs, separated

1½ cups sugar

1½ cups all-purpose flour (spooned into cup and leveled off)

1 teaspoon baking soda

¼ teaspoon salt

12 tablespoons (1½ sticks) unsalted butter, at room temperature

4 ounces German's sweet chocolate, melted

1 teaspoon pure vanilla extract

1 cup plus 2 tablespoons buttermilk

To make the cake: Position the racks in the upper and lower thirds of the oven and preheat to 350°F. Coat two 9-inch round cake pans with cooking spray. Line the bottoms with parchment or waxed paper. Coat the paper with cooking spray.

In a bowl, with an electric mixer, beat the egg whites on medium speed until foamy. Gradually, about 1 tablespoon at a time, add ¾ cup of the sugar, beating until stiff, glossy peaks form. (If you're working with a stand mixer and only have one mixer bowl, transfer the whites to another bowl.)

In a small bowl, whisk together the flour, baking soda, and salt. In a bowl, with an electric mixer, beat together the butter and the remaining ¾ cup sugar on medium speed until light and fluffy. Beat in the egg yolks, one at a time, until well combined. Add in the chocolate and vanilla. Alternately add the flour mixture and the buttermilk beginning and ending with the flour mixture.

Stir about half of the egg whites into the chocolate batter, then gently fold in the remaining egg whites. Divide the batter evenly between the two pans and tap the pans on a work surface to get rid of any air bubbles. Bake on two racks of the oven for 35 to 45 minutes, or until the cake starts to pull away from the sides of the pan and a wooden pick inserted in the center comes out with just a few moist crumbs attached. Let cool in the pans on a wire rack for 10 minutes, then invert the cake (right side up) onto the rack to cool completely. Pull off the paper.

(continued)

Notes

FROSTING

¾ cup cream of coconut
(not coconut cream or
coconut milk)

¾ cup heavy cream

¾ cup granulated sugar

4 large egg yolks

9 tablespoons unsalted butter,
cut into bits

2 cups sweetened shredded
coconut

1½ cups chopped pecans

To make the frosting: In a large, heavy-bottom saucepan, whisk together the cream of coconut, heavy cream, sugar, egg yolks, and butter. Cook over medium heat, whisking constantly, for 10 to 12 minutes, or until thickened and the color of caramel. Remove from the heat and stir in the shredded coconut and pecans and let cool to room temperature.

To assemble the cake: Frost the first layer. Top with the second layer and frost it (don't worry if the frosting dribbles down the sides). Leave the sides unfrosted.

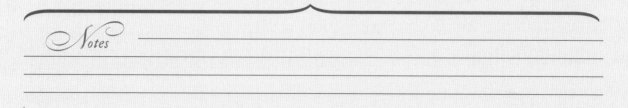

Notes

THE KITCHEN AT
BEEKMAN FARM

GINGERBREAD COOKIE
ICE CREAM SANDWICHES

inger is such a ubiquitous taste during the holiday season that we've often tried to find ways to make it more interesting. One of our most successful experiments came from trying to give our cookie the same kick we got from biting into raw slices of ginger. The combo of ground ginger and mustard powder do the job. We've made ice cream sandwiches with these cookies, but they're equally delicious on their own.

2¼ cups all-purpose flour (spooned into cup and leveled off)

2 teaspoons baking soda

1 tablespoon ground ginger

1 teaspoon ground cinnamon

½ teaspoon ground allspice

½ teaspoon mustard powder

½ teaspoon salt

12 tablespoons (1½ sticks) unsalted butter, at room temperature

½ cup packed light brown sugar

1 cup granulated sugar

⅓ cup molasses (not blackstrap)

1 large egg

1 cup of your favorite ice cream, softened

Preheat the oven to 350°F. Line 2 baking sheets with parchment paper.

In a bowl, whisk together the flour, baking soda, ginger, cinnamon, allspice, mustard powder, and salt.

In a bowl, with an electric mixer on medium speed, beat the butter until soft. Add the brown sugar and ½ cup of the granulated sugar and beat until light and fluffy. Add in the molasses and then the egg, beating well after each is added. Gradually mix in the flour mixture.

Put the remaining ½ cup granulated sugar in a bowl. Using a scant ¼ cup or a #20 ice cream scoop, drop the dough into the bowl and roll to coat. Place the cookies on the baking sheets, spacing them 3 inches apart and flattening them slightly.

Bake for 12 minutes, or until the edges are set and the tops have puffed and then collapsed. Remove from the oven and let cool on the baking sheets.

Spoon 2 tablespoons of ice cream onto 8 cookies and top with the remaining 8 cookies, pressing to seal. Serve or wrap individually and freeze for up to a week.

Notes

FIGGY PUDDING

In the Queen's English, à la mode means "to be fashionable," not "topped with ice cream." A "biscuit" to a Brit is a cookie or a cracker, not a fluffy white bread. And in Britain a figgy "pudding" isn't a soft, spoonable dessert, it's a dense, sweet cake (think plum pudding) whose flavors will remind you of Christmas. As the song says, "bring us some figgy pudding and bring it right here!"

Softened butter for the pan

1½ cups water

¾ pound plump dried figs, stems removed, cut into small bits

3 tablespoons orange liqueur

1½ cups all-purpose flour (spooned into cup and leveled off)

1 tablespoon unsweetened cocoa powder

2¼ teaspoons baking powder

1 teaspoon ground cinnamon

1 teaspoon ground ginger

½ teaspoon freshly grated nutmeg

½ teaspoon salt

3 large eggs

⅔ cup granulated sugar

⅓ cup packed light brown sugar

8 tablespoons (1 stick) unsalted butter, melted

1½ cups fresh bread crumbs (white or whole wheat)

Ice cream or whipped cream, for serving (optional)

Preheat the oven to 350°F. Generously butter an 8- to 10-cup tube pan or metal steamed pudding mold with a top.

In a small saucepan, combine the water and figs. Bring to a boil over high heat, reduce to a bare simmer, cover, and cook for 20 minutes, or until the figs are very tender. Remove from the heat, but don't drain. Stir in the orange liqueur.

In a medium bowl, whisk together the flour, cocoa, baking powder, cinnamon, ginger, nutmeg, and salt.

In a bowl, with an electric mixer, beat together the eggs and granulated and brown sugars until well combined. Beat in the butter and bread crumbs. Stir in the figs and soaking liquid. Fold in the flour mixture. Scrape the batter into the pan. If using a tube pan, cover the top with a double thickness of foil and place a pot lid that will fit snugly on top. If using a steamed pudding mold, close the top.

Place the pan in a roasting pan and pour hot water to come halfway up the sides of the pan. Bake for 2 hours, or until the pudding is firm and starts to pull away from the sides of the pan.

Remove the pan from the water bath and cool on a wire rack for 5 minutes. Run a spatula around the sides and center tube and invert the pudding onto a serving platter. Serve warm with ice cream or whipped cream, if desired.

Notes

CANDIED CITRUS ZEST

MAKES ABOUT 2 CUPS

Candied citrus zest is wonderful to have on hand. It's perfect after dinner or can be used as a garnish. Serve some along with a slice of our Creamsicle Angel Food Cake (page 93) or just nibble on it. The same process can be used for making tangerine, lime, lemon, or grapefruit zest.

3 oranges

1½ cups water

1¼ cups granulated sugar, plus more for coating

3 tablespoons light corn syrup

With a swivel-bladed vegetable peeler, remove the zest from the oranges in wide strips and halve them lengthwise. Reserve the fruit for another use.

In a small pot of boiling water, cook the orange zest for 10 minutes. Drain, then boil in fresh water for 10 minutes. Drain and taste for bitterness. If the zest is still bitter and not tender, blanch for another 10 minutes and drain.

In a medium saucepan, combine the 1½ cups water, sugar, and corn syrup and bring to a boil over high heat. Add the blanched zest and reduce to a simmer. Cover and cook for 30 minutes, or until the zest is translucent and the syrup is reduced to a couple of tablespoons.

With a fork, lift the zest to a bowl, sprinkle with some sugar, and toss to coat. Transfer to a wire rack to dry. Once dry, you can pack the zests in an airtight container where they'll keep for several months.

Notes

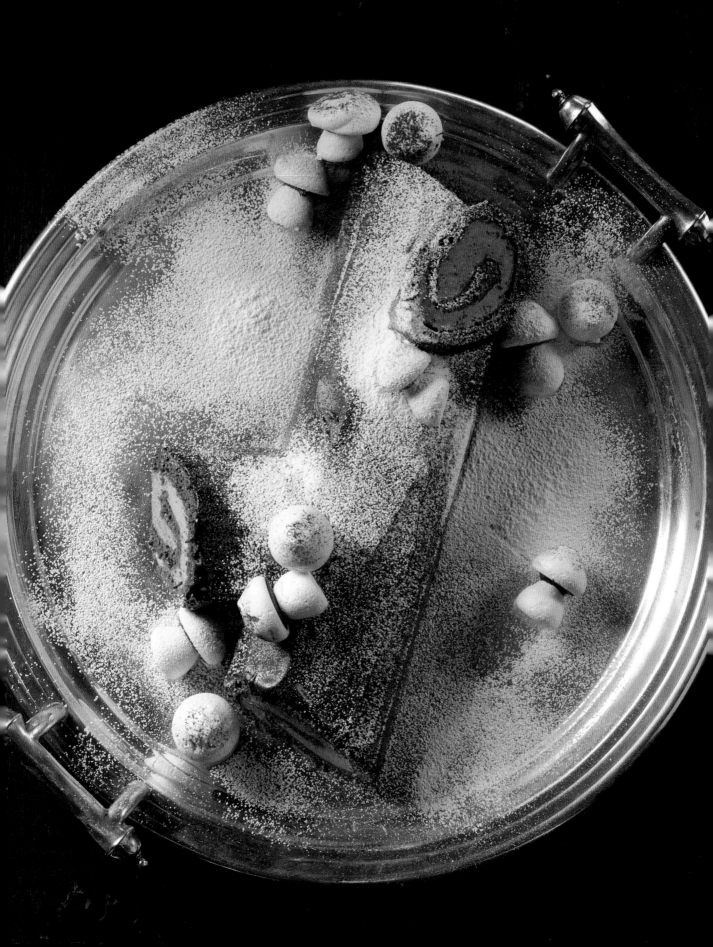

YULE LOG

hink of dessert as the centerpiece of your holiday table. Yule logs are traditionally served at Christmastime. Decorated with Mushroom Meringues (page 60), they look like a log in the forest. Using this bûche de Noël (the classic name for this dessert) as a centerpiece saves you time. You can give the hot glue gun a rest.

CAKE

Softened butter and all-purpose flour for the pan

¼ cup confectioners' sugar

3 large eggs

3 large egg yolks

1½ teaspoons pure vanilla extract

⅛ teaspoon salt

½ cup granulated sugar

⅓ cup all-purpose flour (spooned into cup and leveled off)

⅓ cup cornstarch

¼ cup unsweetened cocoa powder

FILLING

2 tablespoons raspberry liqueur (such as crème de framboise)

2 tablespoons cold water

1 envelope (¼ ounce) plain unflavored gelatin

1 package (10 ounces) frozen unsweetened raspberries, thawed

⅓ cup seedless raspberry jam

1 cup heavy cream

¼ cup sugar

To make the cake: Preheat the oven to 350°F. Butter a 10 × 15-inch jelly-roll pan. Line with waxed paper. Butter and flour the paper. Place a large kitchen towel on a work surface. Dust the towel with the confectioners' sugar.

In a large metal bowl (or the bowl of a stand mixer), whisk together the whole eggs, egg yolks, vanilla, and salt until combined. Gradually whisk in the granulated sugar. Place the bowl over, not in, a pan of simmering water and whisk (by hand) until the mixture is warm (about 115°F on an instant-read thermometer).

Transfer the bowl to the electric mixer fitted with the whisk attachment and beat on medium speed for 4 minutes, or until thick, light in color, and about tripled in volume.

In a small bowl, combine the flour, cornstarch, and cocoa powder. With a strainer, sift one-third of the flour mixture over the egg mixture and gently fold it in by hand. Repeat two more times.

Scrape the mixture into the jelly-roll pan and, with a small offset spatula, evenly spread the batter in the pan. Bake for 9 to 10 minutes, or until the top springs back when lightly touched. Immediately turn the cake onto the kitchen towel and carefully peel off the waxed paper. Starting at one short end, roll up the cake and towel together. Let cool on a wire rack.

To make the filling: In a small bowl, combine the liqueur and cold water. Sprinkle the gelatin over it and let stand for 5 minutes, or until softened.

In a food processor, combine the raspberries and jam and puree. Strain the puree through a fine-mesh sieve and discard the seeds. Transfer the puree to a small saucepan and heat over low heat. Add the gelatin mixture, stirring until melted. Let cool to room temperature.

In a bowl, with an electric mixer, beat the cream and sugar until stiff peaks form. Fold in the raspberry mixture. Refrigerate, whisking occasionally, for 30 minutes, or until it's beginning to set up but still spreadable.

Unroll the cake and spread the raspberry mixture over the cake, leaving a 2-inch border all around. Starting at one short end, roll the cake up jelly-roll fashion.

CHOCOLATE GLAZE

4 ounces bittersweet chocolate,
  melted

5 tablespoons unsalted butter

2 tablespoons honey

Mushroom Meringues (page 60),
  for decorating

Confectioners' sugar for dusting,
  optional

To make the chocolate glaze: In a small saucepan, combine the chocolate, butter, and honey and cook over low heat until melted, stirring until smooth. Scrape into a bowl and let cool until of a spreading consistency.

To assemble the cake: Cut off about 1½ inches from each end of the cake on a shallow angle and set the pieces aside. Spread the glaze on the cake. Place the reserved pieces of cake on the top of the "log," angled side down and spread with the glaze. Refrigerate until set and decorate with Mushroom Meringues. Dust with confectioners' sugar, if desired.

Notes

MUSHROOM MERINGUES

o mushrooms in these—they just look like them. If you've got a wooden mushroom box (you can sometimes find these in supermarkets), line it with a decorative cloth and fill it with the meringues. These are the perfect garnish for the Yule Log (page 58).

2 large egg whites, at room temperature

Pinch of salt

¼ teaspoon cream of tartar

½ cup sugar

½ teaspoon pure vanilla extract

2 teaspoons unsweetened cocoa powder

½ ounce bittersweet chocolate, melted

Preheat the oven to 200°F. Line a large baking sheet with parchment paper.

In a bowl, with an electric mixer, beat the egg whites and salt until foamy. Add the cream of tartar and beat until soft peaks form. Gradually, about 1 tablespoon at a time, add the sugar, beating for 15 minutes, or until stiff, glossy peaks form, adding in the vanilla halfway through.

Fill a pastry bag fitted with a plain ½-inch tip with the meringue and pipe 18 rounds, about the size of a quarter, onto the parchment paper at one end of the baking sheet. (This is for the mushroom caps.) To make the stems, hold the pastry bag upright (perpendicular to the paper) and about an inch above the paper. Squeeze out meringue as you pull up on the pastry bag until the meringue is about 2 inches tall, making it slightly wider at the base. Place the cocoa in a small sieve and sprinkle it over the meringue.

Bake for 1 hour 30 minutes, or until the meringues are crisp and set. Let cool on the baking sheet, then lift off the parchment. With a small icing spatula, spread the flat side of the mushroom caps with the melted chocolate and then "glue" the stems to the caps by pressing the flat side of the stems to the chocolate side of the caps. Store in an airtight container for up to several weeks.

Notes

WINTER HEIRLOOM RECIPE FROM YOUR FAMILY

_____

_____

_____

_____

_____

_____

_____

_____

_____

_____

_____

_____

_____

_____

_____

_____

_____

_____

_____

Spring

Spring

DO-IT-ALL YELLOW CAKE *73* ℚ RUGELACH *74*

COCONUT CAKE *77* ℚ KEY LIME PIE *81*

STRAWBERRY SHORTCAKE WITH BALSAMIC SYRUP *83*

HELLO DOLLIES *85* ℚ LEMON-TOASTED POPPY SEED CAKE *89*

CREAMSICLE ANGEL FOOD CAKE *93* ℚ MINT BARS *97*

BANANA CAKE WITH CREAM CHEESE FROSTING *98*

ROASTED RHUBARB CRISP *101*

PEANUT BUTTER SANDWICH COOKIES *102*

OLIVE OIL POUND CAKE *105* ℚ CHOCOLATE CREAM PIE *108*

THREE-CITRUS CRÈME CARAMEL *109*

CARDAMOM CAKE WITH COFFEE GLAZE *111*

STAINED GLASS GELATIN "CAKE" *113* ℚ BOSTON CREAM PIE *114*

TOASTED COCONUT RICE PUDDING WITH MANGO SAUCE *116*

VANILLA PASTRY CREAM *117*

DOUBLE CHOCOLATE PUDDING *119* ℚ CHOCOLATE ÉCLAIR PIE *121*

CRUSTLESS RICOTTA CHEESECAKE *124*

GRAHAM CRACKERS *125*

DIABLO FOOD CAKE WITH CUSTARD SAUCE *129*

PISTACHIO-CHIP ICE CREAM *130*

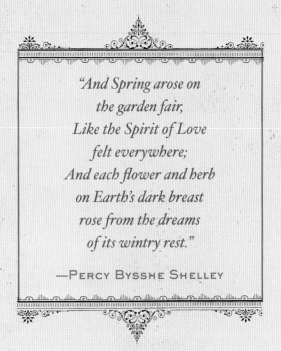

> *"And Spring arose on*
> *the garden fair,*
> *Like the Spirit of Love*
> *felt everywhere;*
> *And each flower and herb*
> *on Earth's dark breast*
> *rose from the dreams*
> *of its wintry rest."*
>
> —PERCY BYSSHE SHELLEY

Spring is about awakening—of color, of sounds of tastes, and scents.

And we flee out the screen doors of the farmhouse to gather as many fresh things as possible: milk from the kidding goats, eggs from the new chickens, rhubarb from the garden, and any berry we can coax from a bush or a vine.

While summer may take all the glory, spring for us takes the cake.

DO-IT-ALL YELLOW CAKE

ossibly the only cake recipe you will ever need and so simple you can commit it to memory! This makes two 9-inch round yellow cakes, the kind your mom might have used for your birthday cake or another celebration. We use it for our Boston Cream Pie (page 114), but you could also fill it with Double Chocolate Pudding (page 119), or place one layer in a springform pan, spread it with ice cream, top with another layer, and freeze for an ice cream cake.

Cooking spray

2 cups cake flour (spooned into cup and leveled off), sifted

2 teaspoons baking powder

1/2 teaspoon salt

10 tablespoons unsalted butter, at room temperature

1 cup plus 2 tablespoons sugar

3 large eggs

3/4 cup milk

1 1/2 teaspoons pure vanilla extract

Grated zest of 1 lemon

Position the racks in the upper and lower thirds of the oven and preheat to 350°F. Coat two 9-inch round cake pans with cooking spray. Line the bottoms with parchment or waxed paper. Coat the paper with cooking spray.

In a bowl, whisk together the flour, baking powder, and salt.

In a bowl, with an electric mixer on medium speed, beat the butter and sugar until light in texture. Add the eggs, one at a time, beating well after each addition.

In a small bowl, stir together the milk, vanilla, and lemon zest. Alternately beat the flour mixture and the milk mixture into the butter mixture, beginning and ending with the flour mixture. Scrape the batter into the pans.

Bake for 25 minutes, or until the cakes start to pull away from the sides of the pans and a wooden pick inserted into the center of the cakes comes out clean. Let cool in the pans on a wire rack for 10 minutes, then run a metal spatula around the sides to loosen the cakes and invert (right side up) onto the rack to cool completely. Pull off the paper.

Notes

RUGELACH

Traditionally, rugelach is a filled pastry made with a cream cheese dough. Here, we use store-bought puff pastry, which makes them come together quickly. Feel free to substitute walnuts for the pecans and chopped dried cherries, raisins, or apricots for the currants. Store in an airtight container for up to a week.

All-purpose flour for the work surface

1 sheet frozen puff pastry (from a 17.3-ounce package), thawed

½ cup granulated sugar

1 tablespoon ground cinnamon

4 tablespoons (½ stick) unsalted butter, melted

½ cup finely chopped pecans

⅓ cup dried currants

1 large egg yolk

1 tablespoon water

Preheat the oven to 350°F. Line a large baking sheet with parchment paper.

On a lightly floured work surface, roll the sheet of puff pastry to a 12 × 15-inch rectangle.

In a small bowl, combine the sugar and cinnamon. Brush the sheet of puff pastry with the butter and sprinkle with the cinnamon-sugar. Scatter the pecans and currants over the top. Cut the pastry sheet into 20 squares (4 across and 5 down). Roll each square up like a log and place seam side down on the baking sheet.

In a small bowl, blend the egg yolk and water. Brush each rugelach with the egg wash and bake for 25 to 30 minutes, or until crisp and golden brown. Transfer to a wire rack to cool completely.

Notes

RADIANCE TOFFEE

THE SPICE CABINET AT
BEEKMAN FARM

COCONUT CAKE

his glorious Southern favorite—a wonderful combination of coconut and lemon— is always on the Easter dinner table at Brent's family's house. Make the Lemon Curd (page 22) ahead of time or buy it prepared.

CAKE

Cooking spray

2¼ cups all-purpose flour (spooned into cup and leveled off)

2½ teaspoons baking powder

½ teaspoon salt

12 tablespoons (1½ sticks) unsalted butter, at room temperature

1⅓ cups granulated sugar

5 large egg whites

1½ teaspoons pure vanilla extract

⅔ cup milk

1 cup Lemon Curd (page 22)

FROSTING

3 large egg whites

1 cup granulated sugar

1 tablespoon light corn syrup

¼ cup water

¼ teaspoon cream of tartar

⅛ teaspoon salt

1½ teaspoons pure vanilla extract

1½ cups sweetened shredded coconut

To make the cake: Position the racks in the upper and lower thirds of the oven and preheat to 350°F. Coat two 8-inch round cake pans with cooking spray. Line the bottoms with parchment or waxed paper. Coat the paper with cooking spray.

In a large bowl, whisk together the flour, baking powder, and salt. In a bowl, with an electric mixer, beat the butter and sugar until light and fluffy. Mix in the egg whites and vanilla until well combined. Alternately add in the flour mixture and the milk, beginning and ending with the flour. Scrape the batter into the pans.

Bake for 35 to 40 minutes, or until the cakes are set around the edges, golden brown, and spring back when lightly touched. Let cool in the pans on a wire rack for 15 minutes, then run a metal spatula around the sides of the cakes and invert onto the racks (right side up) to cool completely. Pull off the paper.

Place one layer on a cake plate and spread with the Lemon Curd. Top with the second layer.

To make the frosting: In a large heatproof bowl set over, not in, a pan of simmering water, combine the egg whites, sugar, corn syrup, water, cream of tartar, and salt. With a handheld mixer, beat on high speed for 7 minutes, or until stiff peaks form. Remove from the heat, add in the vanilla, and continue beating for 5 minutes, or until cool.

Using a long icing spatula, frost the top and sides of the cake. Sprinkle the coconut over the top of the cake and pat it gently onto the sides.

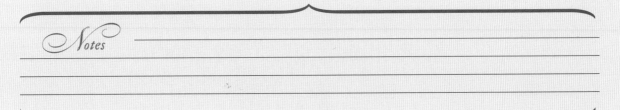

Notes

KEY LIME PIE

ey limes are tarter than Persian limes (regular limes) but often difficult to find. To make a reasonable facsimile, use ½ cup regular lime juice plus 3 tablespoons lemon juice to replace the Key lime juice here.

CRUST

10 full graham cracker sheets

4 tablespoons (½ stick) butter, melted

¼ cup sugar

1 teaspoon grated lime zest

¼ teaspoon salt

FILLING

3 large egg yolks

1 can (14 ounces) sweetened condensed milk

⅔ cup fresh Key lime juice (about 20 Key limes)

MERINGUE

3 large egg whites

Pinch of salt

¼ teaspoon cream of tartar

⅓ cup granulated sugar

¼ teaspoon pure vanilla extract

To make the crust: Preheat the oven to 350°F.

In a food processor, pulse the graham crackers until finely ground. Add the butter, sugar, lime zest, and salt and process until well combined. Press the mixture into the bottom and up the sides of a 9-inch tart pan with a removable bottom. (This is easily done by using a flat-bottomed measuring cup and pressing it into the pan.) Bake for 10 minutes, or until crisp and set. (Leave the oven on.)

To make the filling: Meanwhile in a bowl, with an electric mixer, beat the egg yolks until fluffy. Gradually add the condensed milk and beat until thick. Beat in the lime juice.

Pour the filling mixture into the baked crust and return to the oven to bake for an additional 10 minutes, or until just set. Transfer to a wire rack to cool slightly. Increase the oven temperature to 450°F.

To make the meringue: In a bowl, with an electric mixer, beat the egg whites and salt until foamy. Add the cream of tartar and beat until soft peaks form. Gradually, about 1 tablespoon at a time, add the sugar, beating until stiff, glossy peaks form, adding in the vanilla toward the end. Scoop the meringue onto the lime filling, making swoops with a spatula. Bake for 5 minutes, or until the meringue is set and browned in spots. Cool to room temperature. Serve at room temperature or chilled.

 Notes

STRAWBERRY SHORTCAKE WITH BALSAMIC SYRUP

As long as Mother Nature cooperates, this is the dessert we make and serve in early June. Getting out to the garden before the birds spot the berries is an epic race.

SHORTCAKE

Softened butter for the pan

1½ cups all-purpose flour
   (spooned into cup and
   leveled off)

3 tablespoons granulated sugar

2¼ teaspoons baking powder

½ teaspoon baking soda

½ teaspoon salt

4 tablespoons (½ stick) cold
   unsalted butter, cut into bits

¾ cup plus 2 tablespoons
   buttermilk

BERRIES

1¼ pounds strawberries, hulled
   and halved lengthwise

3 tablespoons granulated sugar

1½ teaspoons balsamic vinegar

Pinch of pepper

(continued)

To make the shortcake: Preheat the oven to 425°F. Butter a 9-inch round cake pan.

In a large bowl, whisk together the flour, sugar, baking powder, baking soda, and salt. Add the butter and with a pastry blender or 2 knives used scissor-fashion, cut in the butter until pea-size bits are formed. Add the buttermilk and mix just until combined. Don't overmix.

Pat the shortcake dough into the pan. Cover the pan with foil. Bake for 12 minutes, then uncover and bake for 5 to 7 minutes, or until firm.

To prepare the berries: In a large bowl, using a potato masher or a spoon, mash ½ pound of the strawberries to a coarse mash. Slice the remaining berries and add to the mash along with the sugar, vinegar, and pepper. Let stand for 20 minutes. Reserving the juices, drain the berries.

To make the topping: In a large bowl, with an electric mixer, whip the cream with the yogurt and sugar until stiff peaks form.

To assemble the dessert: Place the shortcake on a cake plate and top with the berries and whipped cream. Drizzle the reserved juices on top.

Notes

TOPPING

¾ cup heavy cream

2 tablespoons whole-milk Greek yogurt

3 tablespoons granulated sugar

TIP: *Baking the cake covered with foil prevents it from getting a hard crust so the berry juices are more easily absorbed.*

Notes

HELLO DOLLIES

These multilayered bars may be small, but they're rich and addictive! Once made, cool to room temperature and then store in the refrigerator, where they'll keep for about a week. One taste and you'll never want to say good-bye.

1½ cups gingersnap crumbs (from about 6 ounces cookies)

8 tablespoons (1 stick) unsalted butter, melted

2 cups (12 ounces) chocolate chips

1 cup sweetened shredded coconut

1 cup pecans, coarsely chopped

½ cup sweetened cream of coconut (not coconut milk or coconut cream) or sweetened condensed milk

Preheat the oven to 350°F.

In a bowl, combine the gingersnap crumbs and butter. Press the mixture into an 8 × 8-inch baking pan. Scatter the chocolate chips over the crust. Top with the coconut and then the pecans. Pour the cream of coconut over the top.

Bake for 45 minutes, or until the top is lightly browned and set. Cool in the pan on a wire rack. Cut into squares.

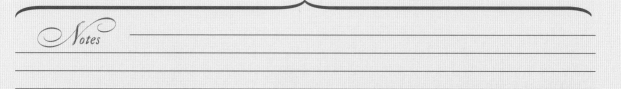

Notes

LEMON-TOASTED POPPY SEED CAKE

f you've ever walked into a deli in New York City, you've seen slices of lemon poppy seed pound cake tempting you from a basket sitting right next to the register. It's an "impulse" buy that's almost impossible to resist. We've even used slices of this cake to make a fabulous French toast.

CAKE

Cooking spray

⅓ cup poppy seeds

12 tablespoons (1½ sticks) unsalted butter, at room temperature

Grated zest of 1 lemon

1 cup whole-milk Greek yogurt

1¾ cups all-purpose flour (spooned into cup and leveled off)

1 teaspoon baking powder

1 teaspoon baking soda

½ teaspoon salt

1 cup granulated sugar

2 large eggs

SYRUP

⅔ cup fresh lemon juice

⅔ cup granulated sugar

To make the cake: Preheat the oven to 350°F. Coat a 9-inch round cake pan with cooking spray. Line the bottom with parchment or waxed paper. Coat the paper with cooking spray.

In a small skillet, toast the poppy seeds over low heat for 3 minutes, or until fragrant. Add the butter and heat until melted. Stir in the lemon zest. Let cool to room temperature. Whisk in the yogurt.

In a medium bowl, whisk together the flour, baking powder, baking soda, and salt.

In a bowl, with an electric mixer, beat the sugar and eggs until light in color. Alternately beat in the flour mixture and the butter mixture, beginning and ending with the flour mixture.

Scrape the batter into the pan and bake for 1 hour, or until the cake starts to pull away from the sides of the pan and a wooden pick inserted in the center comes out with some moist crumbs attached.

To make the syrup: Meanwhile, in a small saucepan, combine the lemon juice and sugar and cook over medium heat, stirring until the sugar has dissolved.

(continued)

Notes

TIP: *If you can get your hands on black sesame seeds, give them a try here. You can use half poppy seeds and half black sesame seeds, or you can use all black sesame seeds, which will give the cake a Middle Eastern flavor.*

Run a metal spatula around the sides of the warm cake and invert it onto a wire rack. Pull off the parchment or waxed paper. Place it right side up onto a cake platter. Using a fork or paring knife, poke several holes in the top. Spoon half the syrup over the cake. Let stand until the syrup has been absorbed, then spoon on the remaining syrup. Serve the cake warm or at room temperature.

Notes

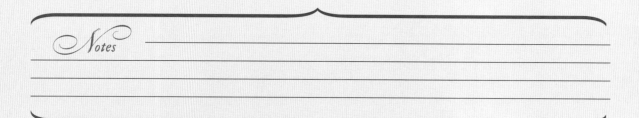

CREAMSICLE ANGEL FOOD CAKE

he flavors of this cake bring to mind a childhood favorite and an American classic: the orange ice and vanilla ice cream pop called a creamsicle. For even more orange flavor, serve with Candied Citrus Zest (page 55).

CAKE

1½ cups granulated sugar

1 cup cake flour (spooned into cup and leveled off), sifted

1½ cups egg whites (from about 12 large eggs)

½ teaspoon salt

1 teaspoon cream of tartar

2 teaspoons pure vanilla extract

Finely grated zest of 1 orange

TOPPING

3 navel oranges

2 tablespoons granulated sugar

To make the cake: Preheat the oven to 325°F. Have a 10-inch ungreased angel food pan ready. (It should not be nonstick.)

In a food processor, process the sugar for 2 minutes, or until finely ground and powdery. Pour half of the sugar into a large bowl and add the flour. Set the remaining sugar aside for the egg whites (next step).

In a bowl, with an electric mixer, beat the egg whites and salt until foamy. Add the cream of tartar and beat until peaks start to form. Gradually, 1 tablespoon at a time, add the reserved finely ground sugar to the egg whites, beating until soft, shiny, droopy peaks form. Mix in the vanilla.

Scatter one-third of the sugar-flour mixture over the egg whites and gently fold in. Repeat with the remaining sugar-flour mixture. Fold in the orange zest.

Spoon the batter into the pan. Bake for 1 hour, or until the top is golden brown and the cake is set.

Immediately invert the cake pan onto the counter. If your pan has feet, simply invert it onto the feet. If it doesn't have feet, invert it onto the neck of a bottle or an upside-down funnel. Let stand until cool, then run a metal spatula around the sides and the center tube of the pan. Run a knife around the bottom to release the cake.

(continued)

Notes

To make the topping: With a paring knife, cut off a thin slice from the bottom of the oranges, then following the curve of the fruit, remove the peel and membranes. Working over a bowl to catch the juice, cut in between the segments to release them from the membranes. Squeeze the membranes to get more juice and transfer to a small saucepan reserving the segment.

Add the sugar to the pan and heat over low heat until the sugar has dissolved. Let cool to room temperature, then stir in the orange segments and chill.

Serve slices of the cake with the oranges and juice alongside.

Notes

MINT BARS

int is one of the first things in the kitchen garden that springs to life. If you're a fan of Girl Scout Thin Mints, these will fast become favorites. Lining the pan with parchment paper enables you to lift the whole bar from the pan easily.

FILLING

2 cups milk

1 cup fresh mint leaves, coarsely chopped

¼ teaspoon salt

½ cup granulated sugar

1 envelope (¼ ounce) plain unflavored gelatin

½ cup heavy cream

2 tablespoons crème de menthe

CRUST

22 Famous Chocolate Wafers

¼ cup granulated sugar

6 tablespoons (¾ stick) unsalted butter, melted

1 mint-flavored chocolate bar (about 1.6 ounces), thinly sliced

To make the filling: In a medium saucepan, combine the milk, mint, and salt and bring to a simmer over medium heat. Remove from the heat, cover, and let steep for 30 minutes.

Strain the milk into a bowl, pushing on the mint to release as much mint flavor as possible. Return the milk to the pan along with the sugar and bring to a simmer. Meanwhile, in a small bowl, sprinkle the gelatin over the cream and let stand for 5 minutes, or until swollen. Add the softened gelatin to the simmering milk and stir until dissolved. Remove from the heat and stir in the crème de menthe. Transfer to a bowl set in a larger bowl of ice and water and stir occasionally for 20 to 30 minutes, or until it starts to thicken.

To make the crust: Meanwhile, preheat the oven to 375°F. Line an 8 × 8-inch baking pan with a double layer of parchment or waxed paper, leaving an overhang on 2 sides.

In a food processor, pulse the wafers and sugar until finely ground. Add the butter and pulse until well combined. Transfer the mixture to the pan, pressing to pack it down. Bake for 8 minutes, or until set.

Set the pan on a wire rack to cool to room temperature.

Pour the mint mixture over the cooled crust. Scatter the chocolate bar pieces over the top and refrigerate until chilled. Use the overhang to lift the bar onto a cutting surface and cut into 12 pieces to serve. Store in the refrigerator.

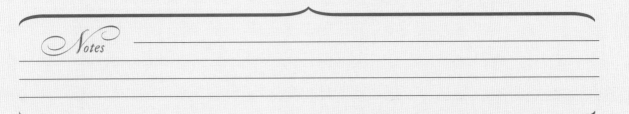

Notes

BANANA CAKE
WITH CREAM CHEESE FROSTING

hrift was a common topic of conversation in Josh's childhood, and his mother could make do with ingredients that other people might have just thrown away. This dessert demonstrates the resourcefulness we try to incorporate into our own kitchen at the farm. Buy bananas a couple of days before you plan on using them so they'll be dead ripe and on their way to being over-ripe for this cake. We like to use a potato masher for mashing the bananas so there are just a few small whole bits of banana left.

CAKE

Softened butter and flour
for the pan

2 cups all-purpose flour
(spooned into cup and
leveled off)

1 teaspoon baking powder

1 teaspoon baking soda

½ teaspoon freshly grated
nutmeg

¼ teaspoon salt

1¼ pounds very ripe bananas,
mashed (1⅓ cups)

2 teaspoons fresh lemon juice

½ cup whole-milk Greek yogurt

12 tablespoons (1½ sticks)
unsalted butter, at room
temperature

To make the cake: Preheat the oven to 350°F. Butter and flour a 9 × 13-inch baking pan. Line the bottom of the pan with parchment or waxed paper. Butter the paper.

In a large bowl, whisk together the flour, baking powder, baking soda, nutmeg, and salt. In a small bowl, combine the mashed bananas and lemon juice. Stir the yogurt into the bananas.

In a bowl, with an electric mixer on medium speed, beat the butter and the granulated and brown sugars together until light and fluffy. Add the eggs, one at a time, beating well after each addition. Beat in the vanilla. With the mixer on low speed, alternately beat in the flour mixture and the banana mixture in 5 additions, beginning and ending with the flour mixture.

Scrape the batter into the pan and bake for 30 to 35 minutes, or until a wooden pick inserted into the center comes out clean with a few moist crumbs clinging to it.

Let cool in the pan on a wire rack. Run a metal spatula around the sides of the cake and invert onto a serving platter (or parchment-lined cookie sheet if you don't have a big enough platter) and pull off the paper.

To make the frosting: In a bowl, with an electric mixer, beat the cream cheese, confectioners' sugar, and yogurt until smooth. Spread on the top of the cake and serve.

Notes

½ cup granulated sugar

½ cup packed light brown sugar

2 large eggs

2 teaspoons pure vanilla extract

FROSTING

2 packages (8 ounces each)
    cream cheese, at room
    temperature

1 cup confectioners' sugar, sifted

⅓ cup whole-milk Greek yogurt

TIP: *When using confectioners'
sugar, be sure to sift it after measuring
to break up the lumps and keep your
frosting smooth.*

ROASTED RHUBARB CRISP

While rhubarb is often paired with strawberries, some of us appreciate this vegetable (yes, it's a vegetable, often called pie plant) for its own tart flavor. It used to be that you could only find it in the spring, but there are now hothouse varieties that are picked almost year-round.

RHUBARB

2 pounds rhubarb, stems
    trimmed, cut into 1-inch
    lengths (about 4 cups)

¾ cup granulated sugar

3 tablespoons all-purpose flour

½ teaspoon ground ginger

1 teaspoon grated orange zest

2 tablespoons orange juice

Pinch of salt

TOPPING

8 ounces vanilla wafers,
    homemade (page 146) or
    store-bought

⅔ cup natural (skin-on) almonds

¼ cup granulated sugar

6 tablespoons (¾ stick) cold
    unsalted butter, cut up

Preheat the oven to 375°F.

To prepare the rhubarb: In a large bowl, toss the rhubarb with the sugar, flour, ginger, orange zest and juice, and salt. Transfer to an 8 × 8-inch baking dish.

To make the topping: In a food processor, combine the wafers, almonds, and sugar and pulse together until coarse crumbs form. Add the butter and pulse until pea-size pieces of crumb-coated butter remain. Scatter the crumb mixture over the rhubarb.

Bake for 35 minutes, or until the rhubarb is tender and the topping is browned and crisp. Serve warm.

Notes

PEANUT BUTTER
SANDWICH COOKIES

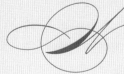*hen it comes to desserts, sometimes more is better. Why have just one peanut butter cookie when you could have two and a delicious peanut butter filling?*

COOKIES

1½ cups all-purpose flour (spooned into cup and leveled off)

¾ teaspoon baking soda

½ teaspoon baking powder

¼ teaspoon salt

1 cup crunchy natural peanut butter

8 tablespoons (1 stick) unsalted butter, at room temperature

¾ cup packed light brown sugar

¼ cup granulated sugar

2 large eggs

1 teaspoon pure vanilla extract

FILLING

⅔ cup crunchy natural peanut butter

4 tablespoons (½ stick) unsalted butter, at room temperature

½ cup confectioners' sugar, sifted

To make the cookies: In a large bowl, whisk together the flour, baking soda, baking powder, and salt.

In a bowl, with an electric mixer, beat the peanut butter and butter together until well combined. Beat in the brown and granulated sugars until light and fluffy. Beat in the eggs, one at a time, beating well after each addition. Beat in the vanilla. With the electric mixer on low speed, beat in the flour mixture. Refrigerate the dough for at least 1 hour or up to overnight, until firm enough to handle.

Position the racks in the upper and lower thirds of the oven and preheat to 375°F. Line 2 baking sheets with parchment or waxed paper.

Roll 2 tablespoons of the dough into a ball, or use a #30 ice cream scoop (1 ounce), and drop the dough 2 inches apart onto the baking sheets. With a fork, flatten the cookies slightly, making a crisscross design on each cookie top.

Bake for 20 minutes, switching the baking sheets from top to bottom and rotating them from front to back halfway through, or until set. Remove from the oven to a wire rack and let cool on the baking sheets.

To make the filling: In a small bowl, beat together the peanut butter, butter, and confectioners' sugar until combined. Spoon a generous tablespoon of filling onto 16 cookies and top with the remaining cookies.

TIP: *Look for "natural" peanut butter without any sugar added. And while we like crunchy, feel free to use creamy if that's your preference.*

Notes

OLIVE OIL POUND CAKE

S o many of the recipes at Beekman 1802 get their start from our memory of watching our moms in the kitchen. These recipes become jumping-off points for our experiments. In this tender, flavorful cake, olive oil takes the place of melted butter, so use an oil with full flavor but no peppery bite.

CAKE

Olive oil for the pan

2 cups cake flour (spooned into cup and leveled off), sifted

½ teaspoon baking powder

½ teaspoon salt

1 cup extra-virgin olive oil

2 teaspoons grated lemon zest

2 teaspoons grated orange zest

2 tablespoons fresh lemon juice

2 tablespoons fresh orange juice

4 large eggs, at room temperature

1⅓ cups granulated sugar

GLAZE

¾ cup confectioners' sugar

1 tablespoon fresh lemon juice

Grated lemon zest, for garnish (optional)

To make the cake: Preheat the oven to 350°F. Oil the bottom and sides of a 9 × 5-inch loaf pan. Line the bottom with parchment or waxed paper. Oil the paper.

In a bowl, whisk together the flour, baking powder, and salt. In a separate bowl, whisk together the oil, lemon zest, orange zest, lemon juice, and orange juice.

In a bowl, with an electric mixer, beat the eggs and granulated sugar for about 7 minutes, or until thick and pale and the mixture forms a ribbon when the beater is lifted. Gradually beat in the oil mixture. Then fold in the flour mixture.

Scrape the batter into the pan and bake for 50 minutes to 1 hour, or until a wooden pick inserted into the center comes out clean with some moist crumbs attached. Let cool in the pan, then run a metal spatula around the sides of the cake and invert (right side up) onto a wire rack removing the paper.

To make the glaze: In a small bowl, stir together the confectioners' sugar and lemon juice.

Set the rack with the cake on it over a sheet of waxed paper. Spoon the glaze over the cake. Garnish with some lemon zest, if desired. Let sit for 15 minutes to set the glaze.

Notes
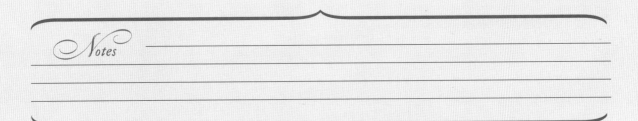

CHOCOLATE CREAM PIE

his was a favorite of Brent's dad, who liked whipped cream instead of the traditional meringue topping. So that's how we do it, too: rich chocolate pudding topped with creamy billows of whipped cream, all packed into a crunchy graham cracker crust. Heaven! If you'd like this to be a triple-chocolate cream pie, you could use Famous Chocolate Wafers in place of the graham cracker crumbs (about 9 ounces crushed in a food processor) and then top the whipped cream with shaved chocolate.

CRUST

1½ cups graham cracker crumbs

3 tablespoons granulated sugar

7 tablespoons butter, melted

FILLING AND TOPPING

Double Chocolate Pudding
    (page 119)

¾ cup heavy cream

2 tablespoons granulated sugar

1 teaspoon pure vanilla extract

To make the crust: Preheat the oven to 375°F.

In a large bowl, stir together the graham cracker crumbs and sugar until combined. Add the butter and stir until the crumbs are well coated. Press the mixture into the bottom and up the sides of a 9-inch pie plate. (This is easily done by using a flat-bottomed measuring cup and pressing it into the pan.) Bake for 10 minutes, or until crisp and set.

To fill the pie: Spoon the pudding into the pie shell, smoothing the top to the edges.

Just before serving, in a bowl, with an electric mixer, beat the cream and sugar until stiff peaks form. Beat in the vanilla. Spoon the whipped cream on top of the pie.

TIP: *You can prepare the pie shell and the Double Chocolate Pudding (page 119) up to 2 days ahead. Keep the pudding in the fridge; the pie shell can be stored at room temp. Top with the whipped cream just before serving.*

Notes _____

_____

_____

_____

THREE-CITRUS CRÈME CARAMEL

here's no dessert so simultaneously light and decadent as crème caramel (or flan, as it's called in Spanish-speaking countries). One of the most seductive aspects of this classic dessert is the dark, sweet flavors of the caramelized sugar that infuses the custard. Though caramelizing sugar may seem like a daunting task, it's really quite easy—and once you've mastered the technique, you'll turn to this elegant dessert again and again.

1 lemon

1 lime

1 navel orange

1½ cups heavy cream

1½ cups milk

⅔ cup plus ¾ cup granulated sugar

½ teaspoon ground cinnamon

¼ teaspoon salt

1 vanilla bean, split lengthwise

1 tablespoon fresh lemon juice

2 large eggs

3 large egg yolks

TIP: *Once the vanilla bean has been used, you can use it again. Simply rinse the bean, let it dry, and use again for a custard or pudding, or simply pop it into the sugar canister where it will give the sugar a slight vanilla flavor.*

With a swivel-bladed vegetable peeler, remove strips of the zest from the lemon, lime, and orange. In a medium saucepan, combine the zests, cream, milk, ⅔ cup of the sugar, the cinnamon, and salt.

Scrape the seeds into the pan and add the vanilla bean. Bring to a gentle simmer over low heat, then remove from the heat, cover, and steep for 30 minutes.

Meanwhile, set out six 1-cup custard cups or ramekins at the ready to be coated with the caramelized sugar. In a large skillet, combine the remaining ¾ cup sugar and lemon juice (which will help keep the sugar from crystallizing) and cook over medium heat without stirring until the sugar has melted and is the color of a brown paper bag. Immediately and carefully pour into the custard cups and then, work quickly, tilt the cups to coat the bottom and sides.

Preheat the oven to 350°F. Line a baking pan large enough to hold the custard cups snugly with a folded-over kitchen towel (this prevents the cups from banging around as they cook) and put a large pot of water on to boil.

In a large bowl, whisk the whole eggs and egg yolks until combined. Strain the milk mixture into the bowl and whisk gently to combine. Place the custard cups in the baking pan and divide the custard among the cups. Place the pan on the pulled-out rack of the oven and pour boiling water into the pan to come halfway up the sides of the cups. Bake for 35 to 40 minutes, or until the custard is just set.

Lift the custards out of the water bath, let cool to room temperature, then refrigerate for 4 to 6 hours, or until chilled. To serve, run a spatula around the edge of the custards, then invert onto serving plates.

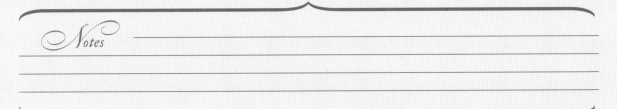

Notes

CARDAMOM CAKE WITH COFFEE GLAZE

 ardamom has a haunting flavor and aroma, floral yet elusive, and here it pairs with pistachio nuts for a Middle Eastern take on a coffee cake.

CAKE

Softened butter for the pan

Fine dried bread crumbs for
the pan

Cooking spray

2⅓ cups cake flour (spooned into
cup and leveled off), sifted

1½ teaspoons ground cardamom

1½ teaspoons baking powder

¾ teaspoon baking soda

½ teaspoon salt

½ cup pistachios

1½ cups plus 2 tablespoons
granulated sugar

8 ounces (2 sticks) unsalted
butter, at room temperature

4 large eggs

1 teaspoon pure vanilla extract

1 cup sour cream

GLAZE

⅔ cup confectioners' sugar

1 teaspoon espresso powder

¼ teaspoon unsweetened
cocoa powder

1 tablespoon milk, plus more
if needed

To make the cake: Preheat the oven to 350°F. Generously butter a 10- to 12-cup Bundt pan. Dust the pan with bread crumbs. Coat with cooking spray.

In a medium bowl, whisk together the flour, cardamom, baking powder, baking soda, and salt. In a food processor, combine the pistachios and 2 tablespoons of the granulated sugar and process until finely ground.

In a bowl, with an electric mixer on medium speed, beat the butter and 1½ cups of the granulated sugar together until light and fluffy. In a small bowl, whisk together the eggs and vanilla. Very gradually add the egg mixture to the butter mixture until very light in texture. Beat in the pistachio-sugar mixture.

With the mixer on low speed, alternately beat in the flour mixture and sour cream, beginning and ending with the flour mixture.

Scrape the batter into the pan and bake for 45 to 55 minutes, or until a wooden pick inserted into the cake comes out clean with some moist crumbs attached. Let cool in the pan on a wire rack, then run a metal spatula around the center and edge of the pan and invert the cake (right side up) onto a cake plate.

To make the glaze: In a small bowl, whisk together the confectioners' sugar, espresso powder, and cocoa powder. Add the milk and stir until of a drizzling consistency, adding a drop or two more of milk if needed. Drizzle over the cake.

Notes

STAINED GLASS GELATIN "CAKE"

SERVES 8

A famous recipe for Crown Jewel Cake, Broken Glass Cake, or Stained Glass Cake appeared on boxes of Jell-O in the 1950s. We've changed the recipe by using fruit juice and unflavored gelatin without losing the visual appeal of several different colors suspended in a white background. It's perfect to bring to a spring or summer potluck. We've chosen pomegranate, pineapple, and (the unexpected) papaya juices, but feel free to swap in whatever flavor or color juice you prefer. This recipe begs for creativity.

5 envelopes (¼ ounce each)
   unflavored gelatin

1½ cups papaya juice

9 tablespoons plus ¾ cup
   granulated sugar

1½ cups pomegranate juice

1½ cups pineapple juice

¾ cup fresh lime juice

¼ cup water

Cooking spray

2 cups cold heavy cream

Have three 8 × 8-inch pans ready.

In a small bowl, sprinkle 1 envelope of gelatin over ½ cup of the papaya juice and let stand for 5 minutes, or until the gelatin is swollen. In a small saucepan, heat the remaining 1 cup papaya juice and 3 tablespoons of the sugar over low heat. Add the softened gelatin and heat until dissolved. Pour into one of the pans and refrigerate for 1 hour, or until gelled.

Repeat with the pomegranate and pineapple juices, using 1 envelope gelatin and 3 tablespoons sugar for each. Pour into separate pans and refrigerate until gelled.

Once the 3 juice gelatins are firm, in a small bowl, combine the lime juice and water and sprinkle the remaining 2 envelopes gelatin over it. Let stand for 5 minutes, or until swollen. Transfer to a small saucepan along with ½ cup of the sugar and heat until the gelatin has melted. Let cool to room temperature.

Coat a 9-inch springform pan with cooking spray.

In a bowl, with an electric mixer, beat the cream and the remaining ¼ cup sugar to soft peaks. Gradually add the cooled lime mixture and beat until firm peaks form. Pour the mixture into the pan and refrigerate for 30 minutes, or until starting to set. Keep an eye on it, and if it's setting too soon take it out of the fridge (it needs to be soft). Meanwhile, cut the 3 pans of juice gelatin into 1-inch cubes.

Gently fold the juice cubes into the cream mixture. Refrigerate for 2 hours, or until set. To serve, release the sides of the pan and cut the "cake" into slices.

Notes

BOSTON CREAM PIE

osh makes this recipe whenever his dad is visiting the farm. Our all-purpose yellow cake is good for all occasions—here, it gets dolled up with pastry cream and a chocolate glaze for a Boston cream pie (OK, you're right, it's a cake). Sandy tells us that this was the first cake she ever made, and it was straight out of a box.

Do-It-All Yellow Cake
    (page 73)
Vanilla Pastry Cream (page 117)

CHOCOLATE GLAZE

3 ounces semisweet chocolate,
    chopped

1 tablespoon light corn syrup

3 tablespoons cold unsalted
    butter, cut into bits

Bake the cake and make the pastry cream.

To make the chocolate glaze: In a double boiler, heat the chocolate and corn syrup over medium heat. Stir until the chocolate has melted. Remove from the heat and whisk in the butter. Set over a larger bowl of ice and water and stir occasionally for 10 minutes, or until it begins to firm up but is still of pouring consistency (or simply leave it on the counter where it will firm up—it'll just take a little longer).

Place one cake layer on a cake plate, flat side up, and spread with the pastry cream. Top with the remaining cake layer and spread the glaze on top, allowing some of the glaze to drip down the sides. Refrigerate for at least 30 minutes to set the glaze.

Notes

TOASTED COCONUT RICE PUDDING WITH MANGO SAUCE

A simple rice pudding in the South includes adding a bit of milk and a bit of sugar to a bit of rice. Many recipes with such simple foundations are the joy of home cooks everywhere because they lend themselves to an infinite number of variations.

1 can (13.5 ounces) coconut milk
   (not cream of coconut)

²/₃ cup long-grain white rice

2 tablespoons light brown sugar

¼ teaspoon salt

¼ cup maple syrup, preferably
   Grade B

²/₃ cup angel flake coconut
   (see Tip below)

1 large mango (about 1 pound),
   cut into ½-inch dice
   (1½ cups)

1 tablespoon fresh lime juice

In a 4-cup glass measure, combine the coconut milk and enough water to equal 4 cups. Transfer to a medium saucepan along with the rice, brown sugar, and salt and bring to a boil over medium heat.

Reduce to a simmer, cover, and cook for 40 minutes, stirring occasionally and checking periodically to see if it needs more water, until the rice is tender. Stir in the maple syrup.

Meanwhile, preheat the oven to 350°F. Place the coconut on a rimmed baking sheet and bake for 10 minutes, or until lightly golden, stirring once or twice.

In a small bowl, toss the mango with the lime juice.

Spoon the pudding into bowls, and serve with the mango and coconut on top.

TIP: *Sweetened flaked coconut is packed in plastic bags and sometimes called angel flake, and can be found in the baking aisle of supermarkets.*

Notes

VANILLA PASTRY CREAM

If you're like us, you can dig into a bowl of pastry cream (very similar to vanilla pudding) and eat the whole thing. Use it to fill a Boston Cream Pie (page 114) or Chocolate Éclair Pie (page 121). Or, you can use it to fill a pie or tart shell and then top it with fresh fruit.

½ cup plus 2 tablespoons
    granulated sugar

2 tablespoons all-purpose flour

2 tablespoons cornstarch

Pinch of salt

6 large egg yolks

2 cups milk

1 teaspoon pure vanilla extract

1 tablespoon unsalted butter

In a large bowl, whisk together the sugar, flour, cornstarch, and salt. Whisk in the egg yolks until smooth.

In a large saucepan, heat the milk over medium-low heat until small bubbles appear around the edge of the pan. Gradually whisk about half of the warm milk into the egg yolk mixture, then whisk the mixture back into the saucepan. Cook, whisking constantly, for 3 to 5 minutes, or until large bubbles erupt on the surface and the pastry cream is thick. Remove from the heat and stir in the vanilla and butter.

Scrape into a bowl. Place a piece of plastic wrap directly on the surface of the pastry cream and cool to room temperature. Refrigerate until chilled.

Notes

DOUBLE CHOCOLATE PUDDING

 *e'd rather have a bowl of this dark, rich chocolate pudding any day instead of chocolate mousse. Serve with a dollop of fresh whipped cream, if you like.*

½ cup granulated sugar

3 tablespoons unsweetened cocoa powder

2 tablespoons cornstarch

½ teaspoon salt

½ teaspoon ground cinnamon

2 large egg yolks

2½ cups milk

4 ounces bittersweet chocolate (60% cacao), coarsely chopped

2 tablespoons unsalted butter

1½ teaspoons pure vanilla extract

Place a fine-mesh sieve over a bowl. In a medium saucepan, whisk together the sugar, cocoa powder, cornstarch, salt, and cinnamon. Whisk in the egg yolks and milk and heat over medium-low heat, whisking constantly, for 5 minutes, or until the pudding starts to bubble and has thickened.

Stir in the chopped chocolate, butter, and vanilla, and stir until melted and smooth. Strain the pudding into the bowl. Place a sheet of plastic wrap directly on the surface of the pudding (unless you like skin on pudding) and let cool to room temperature.

Refrigerate until ready to eat.

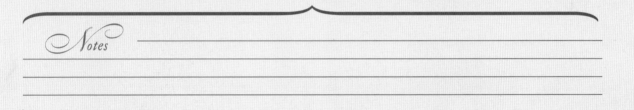

Notes

CHOCOLATE ÉCLAIR PIE

*B*rent remembers his grandma making this; it's a family classic. While the original was made with boxed vanilla pudding, canned chocolate frosting, and processed whipped topping, we've updated it with homemade vanilla pastry cream, a chocolate glaze, and whipped cream. It's perfect for company and completely addictive.

CAKE

Vanilla Pastry Cream (page 117)

¾ cup sour cream

1½ cups heavy cream

⅓ cup granulated sugar

1 box (about 14.4 ounces) graham crackers or double batch of Graham Crackers (page 125)

CHOCOLATE GLAZE

8 ounces semisweet chocolate, coarsely chopped

3 tablespoons light corn syrup

8 tablespoons (1 stick) cold unsalted butter, cut up

To make the cake: Make the pastry cream. Stir the sour cream into the pastry cream and set aside.

In a bowl, with an electric mixer, beat the heavy cream and sugar until stiff peaks form. Stir about a cup of the whipped cream into the pastry cream mixture to lighten it, then gently fold in the remaining whipped cream.

Line the bottom of a 9 × 13-inch baking dish with graham crackers. Top with half the pastry cream mixture, spreading it evenly. Top with another layer of graham crackers and the remaining pastry cream mixture. Top with a final layer of graham crackers.

To make the chocolate glaze: In a large bowl set over, not in, a pan of simmering water, melt the chocolate with the corn syrup. Remove from the heat and whisk in the butter. Set over a larger bowl of ice and water and stir occasionally for 10 minutes, or until it begins to firm up but is still of pouring consistency (or simply leave it on the counter where it will firm up—it'll just take a little longer).

To assemble the pie: Spread the glaze over the graham crackers and refrigerate for at least 8 hours to soften the crackers. Cut into squares (12 to 16) to serve.

*N*otes

CRUSTLESS RICOTTA CHEESECAKE

Every region of the world has its version of the cheesecake. American cheesecake almost always has cream cheese, the Greeks use feta, and German-style includes cottage cheese. Here we've gone with an Italian version using ricotta. It's less dense than American cheesecake but every bit as delicious. It's also super simple.

Softened butter, all-purpose
    flour, and sugar for the pan

1 cup granulated sugar

⅓ cup all-purpose flour

2 pounds ricotta cheese

6 large eggs

1½ teaspoons pure vanilla extract

1 teaspoon grated orange zest

¼ cup pine nuts, toasted

Preheat the oven to 325°F. Butter, flour, and sugar a 9-inch springform pan.

In a large bowl, whisk together the sugar and flour until well combined. Whisk in the ricotta until smooth. Add the eggs, one at a time, until well combined and smooth. Whisk in the vanilla and orange zest. Fold in the pine nuts.

Scrape the batter into the pan and bake for 1 hour, or until set and just slightly wobbly in the center. Let cool in the pan, then refrigerate until chilled. Remove the sides to serve.

TIP: *Check the label on your bag of pine nuts. You might be surprised— some come already toasted. To keep opened toasted pine nuts at their freshest (and this is true of all nuts, toasted or otherwise), place them in the freezer where they'll keep indefinitely.*

Notes

GRAHAM CRACKERS

 *hile store-bought graham crackers are perfectly good and make a quick and easy pie shell, these are really hard to beat.*

1 cup whole wheat flour

¼ cup all-purpose flour

½ cup packed light brown sugar

½ teaspoon baking soda

½ teaspoon salt

3 tablespoons cold unsalted butter, cut into bits

2 tablespoons solid vegetable shortening, chilled

2 tablespoons honey

2 teaspoons molasses (not blackstrap)

2 tablespoons milk

2 tablespoons granulated sugar

In a food processor, pulse the whole wheat and all-purpose flours, brown sugar, baking soda, and salt until combined. Add the butter and vegetable shortening and pulse until the consistency of coarse crumbs.

Add the honey, molasses, and milk and pulse until the dough comes together when pressed between your fingers.

Transfer to a sheet of waxed paper, shape into a rectangle, and refrigerate for at least 30 minutes to firm up.

Preheat the oven to 350°F.

Place the dough between 2 sheets of parchment paper and roll out to a 10 × 12-inch rectangle. Remove the top sheet of parchment paper.

Lift the dough, still on the parchment paper, to a large baking sheet. Cut into thirty 2-inch squares, 5 across and 6 down. Don't separate the crackers. With the tines of a fork, prick the crackers in several spots. Sprinkle the granulated sugar over the top.

Bake for 20 minutes, or until crisp. Immediately cut through the crackers while they're still warm to separate them. Transfer to a wire rack to cool completely.

Notes

DIABLO FOOD CAKE WITH CUSTARD SAUCE

ur twist on devil's food cake, the diablo cake gets a kick from spicy cinnamon, some allspice, and cayenne pepper.

CAKE

Cooking spray

2 cups cake flour (spooned into cup and leveled off), sifted

1 teaspoon baking soda

1/2 teaspoon salt

1/2 teaspoon ground cinnamon

1/8 teaspoon ground allspice

1/8 teaspoon cayenne pepper

2/3 cup unsweetened cocoa powder

1/2 cup water

1 cup buttermilk

2 teaspoons pure vanilla extract

8 tablespoons (1 stick) unsalted butter, at room temperature

1 cup granulated sugar

1 cup packed light brown sugar

2 large eggs

CUSTARD SAUCE

2 cups milk

1/2 cup granulated sugar

3/4 teaspoon ground cinnamon

4 large egg yolks

1/8 teaspoon almond extract

To make the cake: Preheat the oven to 350°F. Coat a 9 × 13-inch baking pan with cooking spray. Line the bottom with parchment or waxed paper. Coat the paper with cooking spray.

In a small bowl, whisk together the flour, baking soda, salt, cinnamon, allspice, and cayenne. In a separate bowl, stir together the cocoa powder and 1/2 cup water. Stir together the buttermilk and vanilla.

In a bowl, with an electric mixer on medium speed, beat the butter and the granulated and brown sugars together until light in texture. Add the eggs, one a time, beating well after each addition. Beat in the cocoa mixture. With the mixer on low speed, alternately add the flour mixture and buttermilk in 3 additions, beginning and ending with the flour mixture.

Scrape the batter into the pan and tap the pan on a countertop to remove any air bubbles. Bake for 35 to 40 minutes, or until a wooden pick inserted in the center comes out with some moist crumbs attached and the cake is beginning to pull away from the sides of the pan. Let cool in the pan on a wire rack. Invert (right side up) on to a cake plate, removing the paper.

To make the custard sauce: Meanwhile, in a medium saucepan, combine the milk, sugar, and cinnamon and bring to a simmer over low heat. In a medium bowl, whisk the egg yolks. Gradually whisk about a cup of the warm milk into the egg yolks, then whisk the warmed eggs back into the pan. Cook, whisking, for 5 minutes, or until the mixture is thick enough to coat a spoon. Remove from the heat and strain through a fine-mesh sieve into a bowl. Stir in the almond extract.

Cut into serving pieces and serve with the custard sauce.

Notes _____

_____

_____

PISTACHIO-CHIP ICE CREAM

When we were little, our grandparents would take us to the local ice cream shop. While we kids would settle for the more pedestrian vanilla and chocolate, the adults always went for the pistachio—its slight green color forever etched in our minds as a mysterious treat only an adult would choose over chocolate. We're happy to let the next generation continue this mythology. More for us! In this recipe, finely ground pistachios give the milk base its pistachio flavor, while crisp roasted pistachios and chocolate chips give it some textural interest and, of course, terrific flavor.

1¼ cups pistachios

1 tablespoon unsalted butter, cut into bits

2½ cups milk

1 cup heavy cream

½ cup granulated sugar

¼ cup honey

¼ teaspoon salt

1 tablespoon plus 2 teaspoons cornstarch

2 ounces semisweet chocolate mini chips

Preheat the oven to 250°F.

In a food processor, finely grind ¾ cup of the pistachios. Set aside.

Place the remaining ½ cup whole pistachios on a small rimmed baking sheet and bake for 50 minutes, or until very crisp. Add the butter, toss, and bake for 10 minutes longer, or until the butter has melted and the nuts are well coated. Set aside.

Meanwhile, in a medium saucepan, combine 2 cups of the milk, the ground pistachios, cream, sugar, honey, and salt and bring to a simmer. Remove from the heat, cover, and let steep for 30 minutes. Strain the milk through a fine-mesh sieve into a bowl and discard the solids. Return the milk mixture to the saucepan and bring to a simmer.

In a small bowl, stir the remaining ½ cup milk into the cornstarch, stirring until no lumps remain. Stir the cornstarch mixture into the simmering milk mixture and cook, stirring constantly, for 1 minute, or until lightly thickened. Remove from the heat and let cool to room temperature.

Transfer the milk mixture to an ice cream machine and process according to the manufacturer's directions, adding the whole toasted pistachios and the chocolate chips during the final minutes of processing. Serve right away or transfer to a freezer container and freeze.

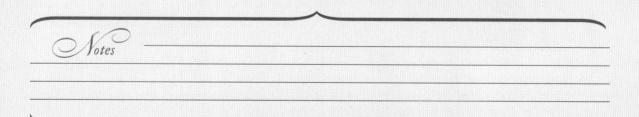

Notes

SPRING HEIRLOOM RECIPE FROM YOUR FAMILY

Summer

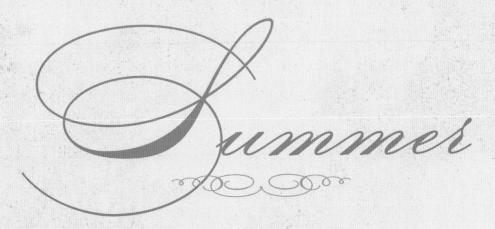

Summer

PLUM UPSIDE-DOWN CAKE *141*

SWEET GREEN TOMATO HAND PIES *142*

BANANA PUDDING WITH VANILLA WAFERS *146*

LEMON LAVENDER SQUARES *153*

ONE-BOWL CHOCOLATE ALMOND CAKE *154*

POACHED PEARS STUFFED WITH GOAT CHEESE *156*

CORNCAKES WITH BUTTERMILK ICE CREAM *157*

GRILLED FRUIT COCKTAIL WITH BOURBON *161*

SYRUP NUTS *162* ❊ SOUR CHERRY STREUSEL PIE *165*

FROZEN HOT CHOCOLATE *167* ❊ BAKED MANHATTAN *169*

BAKED STONE FRUITS WITH CANNOLI CREAM *170*

PEACH COBBLER *173* ❊ BUTTERSCOTCH PUDDING *175*

A TRIO OF ICE CREAM TOPPINGS:

BLUEBERRY, CARAMEL, AND FUDGE *178*

HONEY ICE CREAM *181* ❊ PINK GRAPEFRUIT AND CAMPARI ICE *183*

FRUIT PIZZA WITH SHORTBREAD COOKIE CRUST *184*

BUTTER PECAN ICE CREAM *185* ❊ PEANUT BUTTER ICE CREAM *188*

SUMMER FRUIT IN WINE SYRUP *189* ❊ RED CURRANT JELLY CAKE *191*

BAVARIAN CREAM FRESH FRUIT TRIFLE *194*

IN-A-MINUTE MELON SORBET *195*

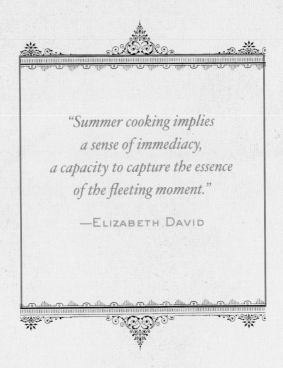

*"Summer cooking implies
a sense of immediacy,
a capacity to capture the essence
of the fleeting moment."*

—ELIZABETH DAVID

As children our moms would send us outside right after breakfast, and we wouldn't come home until the last lightening bug had been caught. On particularly hot days, we might run to the back door for a glass of lemonade served in a frosty aluminum tumbler, or we might beg to turn the hand-cranked ice cream churn (at least for the first few minutes) while sitting in the shade of a tree in the after dinner gloaming.

As long and vibrant as summer days are, they always seem fleeting—even in memory.

On the farm, summer is about making the most of every second. Because tomorrow is not just another day. It's another day less.

PLUM UPSIDE-DOWN CAKE

his is a great "back pocket" recipe. It's one that you can always turn to and is adaptable. Black plums are sweet and juicy, but you can sub in another plum variety, peeled peaches, or any combo of stone fruits.

9 tablespoons unsalted butter, at room temperature

²⁄₃ cup packed light brown sugar

¹⁄₃ cup sliced almonds

¹⁄₄ teaspoon ground allspice

2 black plums (10 ounces total), cut into ¹⁄₂-inch-thick wedges

1¹⁄₄ cups all-purpose flour (spooned into cup and leveled off)

1 teaspoon baking powder

¹⁄₂ teaspoon baking soda

¹⁄₄ teaspoon salt

¹⁄₂ cup granulated sugar

1 large egg

1 teaspoon pure vanilla extract

¹⁄₈ teaspoon almond extract

³⁄₄ cup sour cream

Preheat the oven to 350°F. Place 3 tablespoons of the butter in a 9-inch round cake pan and put it in the oven to melt while the oven preheats. Once melted, carefully tilt the pan to coat the sides.

Sprinkle the brown sugar over the bottom of the pan to evenly coat. Scatter with the almonds and allspice and arrange the plums in a circle on top.

In a large bowl, whisk together the flour, baking powder, baking soda, and salt.

In a bowl, with an electric mixer on medium speed, beat the remaining 6 tablespoons butter and the granulated sugar until light and fluffy. Beat in the egg and the extracts until well combined. Alternately beat in the flour mixture and the sour cream, beginning and ending with the flour mixture, until blended.

Scrape the batter into the pan over the plums and smooth the top. Bake for 35 to 40 minutes, or until a wooden pick inserted in the center comes out clean.

Let cool in the pan for 15 minutes, then run a metal spatula around the side of the cake and invert (right side up) onto a rimmed cake platter. Serve warm or at room temperature.

Notes

SWEET GREEN TOMATO HAND PIES

In the rural South (where Brent grew up), "waste not, want not" was a common utterance. And when faced with a bumper crop on the farm, you had to think creatively so that nothing got wasted. So, tomatoes in a dessert? You bet. The filling for this dessert is a tomato jam, and if you've got any left over, try spreading it on bread or crackers for a great hors d'oeuvre. We've simplified this hand pie recipe by using a quick yogurt dough, which makes for a very flaky and sturdy pocket for the delicious treasure inside. (We've used green tomatoes, but feel free to swap in your favorites.)

DOUGH

1½ cups all-purpose flour
(spooned into cup and
leveled off)

1 tablespoon plus 1 teaspoon
granulated sugar

¼ teaspoon salt

8 tablespoons (1 stick) cold
unsalted butter, cut into bits

½ cup whole-milk Greek yogurt

Flour for the work surface

FILLING

2 green tomatoes (about
10 ounces), cored and
coarsely chopped

1 plum tomato, cored and
coarsely chopped

⅓ cup granulated sugar

½ teaspoon grated orange zest

¼ teaspoon ground cinnamon

⅛ teaspoon salt

2 tablespoons finely chopped
crystallized ginger

1 tablespoon fresh lemon juice

2 tablespoons orange juice

1 tablespoon cornstarch

To make the dough: In a food processor, combine the flour, sugar, and salt and pulse until combined. Add the butter and pulse until the mixture resembles coarse crumbs. Add the yogurt and pulse just until combined (the dough should hold together when pinched between your fingers). Divide the dough in half, transfer to 2 sheets of plastic wrap, and flatten each into a disk. Wrap well and refrigerate for at least 1 hour or up to a day. For longer storage, freeze up to 3 months.

To make the filling: In a medium saucepan, combine the tomatoes, sugar, orange zest, cinnamon, and salt. Bring to a simmer over medium heat, stirring until the sugar has dissolved. Simmer, uncovered, for 15 minutes, or until the tomatoes are very soft and tender. Stir in the ginger and lemon juice and cook for 2 minutes longer to soften the ginger.

In a small bowl, stir the orange juice into the cornstarch until dissolved. Stir the cornstarch mixture into the simmering tomatoes and cook 1 minute, or until thickened. Let cool to room temperature.

Preheat the oven to 325°F. Line a baking sheet with parchment or waxed paper.

Working with half the dough at a time, on a lightly floured work surface, roll the dough to a ⅛-inch thickness. Using a 4½-inch round cutter, cut out 8 rounds, rerolling the scraps if necessary. Spoon a

(continued)

Notes

EGG WASH

1 large egg

1 tablespoon water

TIP: *Both the filling and the dough can be doubled and the entire hand pie can be frozen and then baked without thawing.*

generous tablespoon of filling on the bottom half of each round, leaving a ½-inch border. Brush the border with water, fold the top of the round over, and pinch to seal. Repeat with the remaining dough and filling.

With a small knife, make several shallow crisscross cuts in each hand pie.

To make the egg wash: In a small bowl, beat the egg and water.

Place the hand pies on the baking sheet and brush the tops with the egg wash. Bake for 20 minutes, or until the tops are golden brown and crisp. Transfer to a wire rack to cool for 5 minutes before serving.

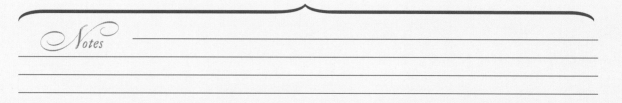

Notes

BANANA PUDDING WITH VANILLA WAFERS

When Brent was growing up in North Carolina, his great-grandmother, Jesse, would make this classic Southern dessert every Easter. These wafers are easy to make, but feel free to swap in store-bought vanilla wafers—you'll need about 30. The dough yields enough for about 5 dozen cookies, but you have choices: Bake all the dough (you'll like these on their own); bake half, forming and freezing the other half to bake at your leisure; or halve the dough ingredients.

VANILLA PUDDING

⅔ cup granulated sugar

¼ cup cornstarch

3 large egg yolks

3 cups milk

2 tablespoons cold unsalted butter

1 teaspoon pure vanilla extract

VANILLA WAFERS

1½ cups all-purpose flour (spooned into cup and leveled off)

1½ teaspoons baking powder

½ teaspoon salt

8 tablespoons (1 stick) unsalted butter, at room temperature

¾ cup granulated sugar

1 large egg

1½ teaspoons pure vanilla extract

2 tablespoons milk

To make the pudding: Set a fine-mesh sieve over a bowl. In a large, heavy-bottom saucepan, whisk together the sugar and cornstarch. Whisk in the egg yolks and milk until smooth. Place the saucepan over medium heat and cook, whisking constantly, for 5 minutes, or until the pudding has thickened and large bubbles erupt on the surface. Transfer the pudding to the sieve and strain. Stir in the butter and vanilla. Place a sheet of plastic wrap directly on the surface of the pudding and refrigerate until chilled.

To make the vanilla wafers: In a small bowl, whisk together the flour, baking powder, and salt. In a bowl, with an electric mixer on medium speed, beat the butter and sugar until well combined. Add the egg, vanilla, and milk and beat until combined. With the mixer on the lowest speed, beat the flour mixture into the butter mixture. Place the dough in the refrigerator to chill for 30 minutes.

Position the racks in the upper and lower thirds of the oven and preheat to 350°F. Line 2 baking sheets with parchment or waxed paper.

Drop the cookie dough in walnut-size balls onto the baking sheets 1 inch apart. With the bottom of a floured drinking glass, flatten the dough slightly. Bake for 15 minutes, switching the baking sheets from top to bottom and rotating front to back halfway through, until golden brown around the edges. Let cool for 2 minutes on the pans, then remove to a wire rack to cool completely.

(continued)

Notes

BANANAS

3 tablespoons granulated sugar

⅓ cup water

3 tablespoons fresh lime juice

1 pound bananas, cut into ¼-inch-
thick slices

To prepare the bananas: In a large skillet, combine the sugar, water, and the lime juice and bring to a boil over medium heat. Boil for 2 minutes, then add the bananas and toss to coat. Remove from the heat.

In a 9 × 9-inch baking dish, make layers of pudding, bananas and their syrup, and vanilla wafers, beginning and ending with pudding. Cover the surface of the pudding with plastic wrap and refrigerate until thoroughly chilled. Alternatively, layer in parfait glases and top with a few wafers.

Notes

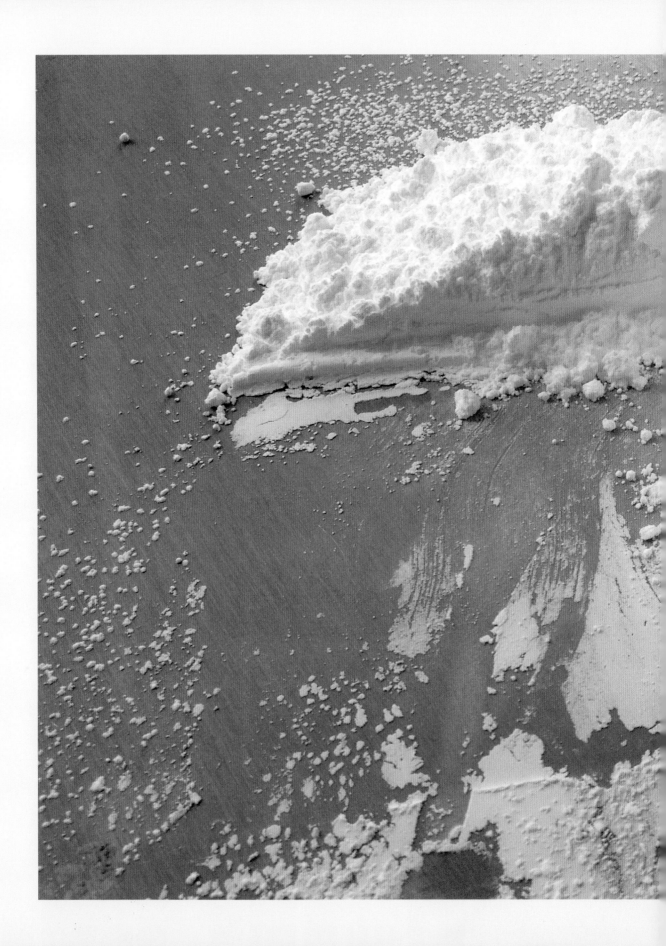

LEMON LAVENDER SQUARES

ook for lavender in the spice section of the supermarket. It gives a slightly floral note to the dessert without being overpowering.

CRUST

¾ cup all-purpose flour (spooned into cup and leveled off)

¼ cup cornstarch

⅓ cup confectioners' sugar

½ teaspoon salt

8 tablespoons (1 stick) cold unsalted butter, cut into bits

¾ teaspoon dried lavender, crumbled

FILLING

3 large eggs

1 large egg yolk

1 cup granulated sugar

Grated zest of 1 lemon

½ cup fresh lemon juice

¼ cup all-purpose flour

¼ teaspoon salt

Confectioners' sugar for dusting

To make the crust: Preheat the oven to 350°F. Line an 8 × 8-inch baking pan with parchment or waxed paper, leaving a 2-inch overhang on two sides.

In a food processor, combine the flour, cornstarch, confectioners' sugar, and salt and pulse until combined. Add the butter and lavender and pulse until the mixture resembles coarse crumbs.

Place the mixture in the pan, cover with plastic wrap, and press the dough in an even layer into the pan and up ½ inch on the sides. Remove the plastic wrap. Bake for 20 to 25 minutes, or until set and golden brown. Leave the oven on but reduce the temperature to 325°F.

To make the filling: Meanwhile, in a bowl, with an electric mixer, beat the whole eggs, egg yolk, and granulated sugar until light. Beat in the lemon zest and lemon juice, flour, and salt until well combined.

Pour the lemon mixture over the warm crust and bake for 20 minutes, or until set. Let cool to room temperature, then refrigerate for at least 1 hour before using the overhang to lift the dessert out of the pan. Dust with confectioners' sugar and cut into 16 rectangles.

Notes

ONE-BOWL CHOCOLATE ALMOND CAKE

ho wants to spend time in the summer cleaning up a lot of dishes? Almonds take the place of flour in this dense chocolate cake. To keep the cake extra fudgy, bake until it's set around the edges but still slightly soft in the center. Warning: There will be fights over who gets to lick this batter bowl!

CAKE

Cooking spray

8 tablespoons (1 stick) unsalted butter, at room temperature

½ cup granulated sugar

3 tablespoons unsweetened cocoa powder

¼ teaspoon salt

3 tablespoons honey

2 tablespoons dark rum

3 large eggs

4 ounces bittersweet chocolate (60% cacao), melted

1 cup natural (skin-on) almonds, finely ground

GLAZE

2 tablespoons honey

3 tablespoons water

¼ cup granulated sugar

3 ounces bittersweet chocolate (60% cacao), coarsely chopped

1 tablespoon cold unsalted butter

To make the cake: Preheat the oven to 375°F. Coat the bottom and sides of an 8-inch round cake pan with cooking spray. Line the bottom with parchment or waxed paper. Coat the paper with cooking spray.

In a bowl, with an electric mixer on medium speed, beat the butter, sugar, cocoa powder, and salt until well combined and light in texture. Beat in the honey and rum. Add the eggs, one at a time, beating well after each addition. Stir in the chocolate and almonds.

Scrape the batter into the pan and bake for 25 minutes, or until a wooden pick inserted in the center comes out with some moist crumbs attached. (The cake will be set around the sides but be slightly fudgy in the center.) Let cool in the pan on a wire rack, then run a metal spatula around the sides of the cake and invert. Pull off the paper and set right side up on a cake platter.

To make the glaze: In a small saucepan, combine the honey and water and bring to a simmer. Add the sugar and chocolate and stir until the chocolate has melted. Remove from the heat, transfer to a bowl, and whisk in the butter, whisking frequently, for 20 to 30 minutes, or until the glaze has thickened but is of a spreading consistency.

Spoon the glaze over the cake, allowing some to drip down the sides. Let stand until set.

TIP: *No need to get blanched (skinned) almonds—almonds with their skin on give the cake a robust flavor.*

Notes

POACHED PEARS
STUFFED WITH GOAT CHEESE

he pear trees on the farm never fail to produce, even when other trees in the heirloom orchard have a lackluster year. They are a welcome sign that the end of summer is arriving, that things are slowing down, and that the chore list will get shorter with the days. Firm Bartletts or Anjous work best here—Boscs will take longer to cook and have a slightly gritty texture. For the nicest presentation, choose pears with their stems intact.

2 cups red wine

¾ cup granulated sugar

8 black peppercorns

1 small cinnamon stick, split

4 firm Bartlett or Anjou pears, peeled and cored from the bottom

2 ounces goat's milk blue cheese

2 ounces soft goat cheese

1 tablespoon milk

In a saucepan wide enough to hold the pears snugly in a single layer on their sides, combine the wine, sugar, peppercorns, and cinnamon stick and heat over medium heat, stirring until the sugar has dissolved. Add the pears lying down, cover with waxed paper (placing it directly on the pears), and simmer, turning the pears over halfway through, for 30 minutes, or until they can be pierced with the tip of a knife. Timing will vary depending on the ripeness of the pears.

Lift the pears out of the poaching liquid and transfer to a container. Bring the liquid to a boil over high heat and boil for 20 minutes, or until reduced to a syrup. Strain and let cool to room temperature. If not serving right away, pour the syrup over the pears and refrigerate.

Halve the pears from top to bottom. In a small bowl, mash together the blue cheese, soft goat cheese, and milk. Spoon the mixture into a pastry bag or a small resealable plastic bag with the corner cut off, and pipe the cheese into the pears. Serve drizzled with the syrup.

Notes

CORNCAKES WITH BUTTERMILK ICE CREAM

e love breakfast, we love pancakes, and we certainly love ice cream. Here they all come together for a warm, country dessert. You can make the corncakes ahead and freeze them, and of course, the ice cream has to be made ahead. To reheat the corncakes, wrap them in foil and place on a baking sheet in a 300°F oven for about 10 minutes, or heat in the microwave.

ICE CREAM

1½ cups heavy cream

½ cup packed light brown sugar

½ cup granulated sugar

1 tablespoon light corn syrup

¼ teaspoon salt

¼ teaspoon freshly grated nutmeg

1 tablespoon cornstarch

2 cups buttermilk

1 teaspoon pure vanilla extract

CORNCAKES

½ cup plus 2 tablespoons cornmeal

3 tablespoons all-purpose flour

2 tablespoons granulated sugar

2 teaspoons baking powder

½ teaspoon salt

⅔ cup milk

2 large eggs

3 tablespoons unsalted butter, melted, plus more for the pan

1¾ cups corn kernels, fresh or thawed frozen

TIP: *If you don't have buttermilk, simply use plain yogurt and thin with a little milk or water.*

To make the ice cream: In a medium, heavy-bottom saucepan, combine 1¼ cups of the cream, the brown and granulated sugars, corn syrup, salt, and nutmeg and bring to a simmer over medium heat. Meanwhile, in a small bowl, dissolve the cornstarch in the remaining ¼ cup cream. Whisk the cornstarch mixture into the simmering cream and cook, stirring constantly, for 1 minute, or until thickened. Remove from the heat, let cool to room temperature, and whisk in the buttermilk and vanilla. Transfer the mixture to an ice cream machine and process according to the manufacturer's directions. Transfer to a freezer container and freeze.

To make the corncakes: Preheat the oven to 200°F.

In a large bowl, whisk together the cornmeal, flour, sugar, baking powder, and salt. In a separate bowl, whisk together the milk, eggs, and butter. Stir into the flour mixture and fold in the corn.

Heat a large nonstick skillet or griddle and brush lightly with melted butter. Drop the batter by 2 tablespoons (you can use a small ice cream scoop for this or measure half of a ¼-cup measure) onto the pan and cook for 2 minutes, or until bubbles appear at the top. Turn the cakes over and cook for 1 minute longer, or until the bottoms are lightly browned. Transfer to a baking sheet and place in the oven to keep warm while you make more corncakes.

Serve the warm corncakes with the cold ice cream.

Notes

GRILLED FRUIT COCKTAIL
WITH BOURBON

ruit cocktail always seemed to be a staple of school lunch menus when we were growing up. Legend went that if you received a serving with the (rare) maraschino cherry half, you would have good luck that day. This is our "adult" version. Feel free to swap in peaches for the nectarines, or just do one type of fruit; it's really up to you. This recipe will help you make the most of the summer farmers' market, and feel free to throw in as many cherries as you want, too!

3 tablespoons bourbon

3 tablespoons light brown sugar

2 tablespoons fresh lime juice

1 tablespoon unsalted butter, melted

2 teaspoons vegetable oil, plus more for the grill topper

1 pound nectarines, quartered

2 black plums (5 ounces each), halved

¾ cup sour cream

In a large bowl or shallow dish large enough to hold the fruit in a single layer, whisk together the bourbon, 1 tablespoon of the brown sugar, the lime juice, butter, and oil. Add the fruit and toss well to coat. Let sit at room temperature for 1 hour or up to 4 hours.

Preheat a grill to medium-low. Oil a grill topper. Lift the fruit from the marinade and reserve the marinade. Grill the fruit, turning it as it softens and colors, for 10 minutes. As each piece of fruit is grilled, return it to the dish with the marinade.

In a small bowl, stir together the sour cream and the remaining 2 tablespoons brown sugar. Serve the fruit with the juices and a dollop of the sweetened sour cream.

Notes

SYRUP NUTS

We love to have a jar of these on hand throughout the summer for those spontaneous ice cream socials on the back porch. You can also spoon them over pancakes or use to top a bowl of sliced bananas and sweetened sour cream.

1 cup mixed unsalted nuts, such as pecans, walnuts, almonds, hazelnuts, and cashews

½ cup granulated sugar

⅓ cup maple syrup, preferably Grade B

1 vanilla bean, split lengthwise

¼ teaspoon salt

¾ cup water

2 tablespoons brandy, Scotch, or bourbon

Preheat the oven to 350°F. Spread the nuts on a rimmed baking sheet and bake for 10 minutes, or until crisp and fragrant.

Meanwhile, in a small saucepan, combine the sugar, maple syrup, vanilla bean, salt, and water and bring to a boil over medium heat.

Add the nuts to the syrup, bring the mixture to a simmer, and cook for 10 minutes.

Let the nuts cool in the syrup, then stir in the brandy. Transfer to a clean jar and refrigerate until ready to use. The syrup nuts can be stored in the refrigerator for up to 3 months.

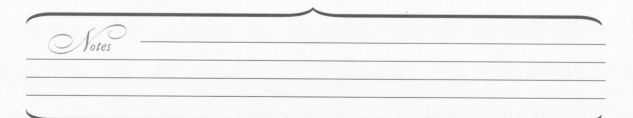

Notes

SOUR CHERRY STREUSEL PIE

very summer begins with a battle with the birds for our fair share from the cherry tree. And this dessert is worth fighting for!

Basic Pie Dough (page 8)

Flour for the work surface

STREUSEL TOPPING

1 cup all-purpose flour (spooned into cup and leveled off)

½ cup packed light brown sugar

8 tablespoons (1 stick) cold unsalted butter, cut into bits

1 teaspoon pure vanilla extract

FILLING

½ cup granulated sugar

¼ cup all-purpose flour

¾ teaspoon ground cinnamon

⅛ teaspoon ground allspice

3 cans (16 ounces each) water-packed pitted sour cherries, drained (about 4 cups)

¼ cup orange juice

To make the crust: Make the pie dough and chill as directed. On a lightly floured work surface, roll out the dough to a 12-inch round. Roll the dough around the rolling pin and then fit it into a 9-inch pie plate without stretching, pressing the dough into the bottom and against the sides of the pan. With a pair of scissors or a paring knife, trim the dough to leave a 1-inch overhang all around. Fold the overhang in over the rim to make a double layer of dough and, with your fingers, crimp the dough around the edge. Refrigerate for at least 1 hour before baking (this helps relax the dough so it doesn't shrink when baking).

To make the streusel topping: Meanwhile, in a medium bowl, combine the flour and brown sugar. Add the butter and vanilla and work the butter into the dry ingredients with your fingers to form large coarse crumbs. Refrigerate until ready to use.

Preheat the oven to 375°F. Place a foil-lined baking sheet on the shelf below the pie to catch drips from the pie.

To make the filling: In a large bowl, whisk together the granulated sugar, flour, cinnamon, and allspice. Add the cherries, tossing well to coat. Add the orange juice.

Pour the mixture into the pie shell and top with the streusel topping. Bake for 1 hour, or until the juices are bubbling, the crust is golden brown, and the streusel topping is crisp. Let cool on a wire rack for at least 1 hour before serving.

TIP: *Because fresh sour cherries have such a short season (early summer, usually June) and they don't ship to that many markets, it's a much more reliable option to use canned or jarred tart cherries. However, if you're lucky enough to get yours hands-on fresh, you'll need about 2 pounds. Just pit them and follow the recipe.*

Notes

FROZEN HOT CHOCOLATE

ust down the street from where we used to live in NYC was a Manhattan culinary landmark called Serendipity. Its most famous concoction was this dessert that falls somewhere between a classic milkshake and a cold glass of rich chocolate milk—we've dolled it up even more by adding hazelnut liqueur. If you prefer, you can add your favorite liqueur or omit the alcohol and increase the milk to 1½ cups.

4 ounces bittersweet chocolate (60% cacao), coarsely chopped

1 tablespoon unsweetened cocoa powder

2 tablespoons dark brown sugar

Pinch of salt

1¼ cups milk

2 tablespoons hazelnut liqueur (optional)

3 cups ice cubes

Whipped cream (optional)

Chocolate shavings (optional)

In a small bowl set over, not in, a pan of simmering water, melt the chocolate.

Meanwhile, in another small bowl, stir together the cocoa powder, brown sugar, and salt. Add ¼ cup of the milk and stir until smooth. Stir in the melted chocolate. Let cool to room temperature.

Transfer the mixture to a blender along with the remaining 1 cup milk, the liqueur (if desired), and ice. Blend until smooth and thick. Divide between 2 large glasses and top with whipped cream and chocolate shavings, if desired.

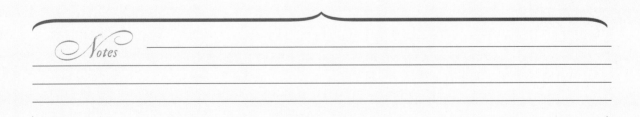

Notes

BAKED MANHATTAN

You can take the boys out of the city, but you can't take all of the city out of the boys. We've always associated the sipping of an ice-cold Manhattan cocktail as a ritual of summer, but you don't have to be an urbanite to appreciate how we've put a cocktail dress on a traditional pound cake. For the best taste, use an all-butter pound cake.

SYRUP

⅓ cup granulated sugar

¼ cup water

2 tablespoons rye, Scotch, or bourbon

CAKE

Cooking spray

1 store-bought all-butter pound cake (11.5 ounces), cut into ½-inch-thick slices

2 pints Cherry Garcia ice cream (or other cherry ice cream), softened

MERINGUE

4 large egg whites

¼ teaspoon salt

½ teaspoon cream of tartar

¾ cup granulated sugar

To make the syrup: In a small saucepan, combine the sugar and water and bring to a boil over medium heat, stirring until the sugar has dissolved. Remove from the heat and stir in the rye.

To assemble the cake: Lightly coat a 9-inch pie plate with cooking spray. Brush both sides of the cake slices with the syrup and line the bottom and sides of the plate with some of the cake.

Spread the ice cream over the cake, covering it completely. Top with the remaining cake slices, cutting pieces to fit. Freeze until solid, at least 8 hours.

Preheat the oven to 500°F.

To make the meringue: In a bowl, with an electric mixer, beat the egg whites and salt until foamy. Add the cream of tartar and beat until soft peaks form. Gradually, about 1 tablespoon at a time, add the sugar, beating until stiff, glossy peaks form. With a spatula, spread the meringue over the cake, covering it to the edges of the pan. Using the spatula, make high swooping peaks. Place on a baking sheet and bake for 2½ to 3 minutes, or until lightly browned on top. Serve immediately.

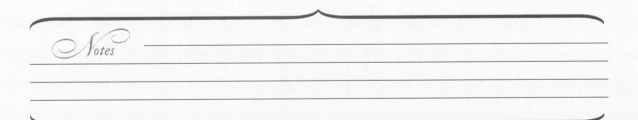

Notes

BAKED STONE FRUITS WITH CANNOLI CREAM

Roasting fruit both concentrates and caramelizes its natural sugars and intensifies its flavor. The sweetened ricotta filling that might normally fill a cannoli adds a nice creaminess to the dish. Adding the bay leaves and a touch of rosemary intensifies the flavors and adds a touch of sophistication to a simple summer dessert.

¾ pound Bing cherries, pitted

2 peaches (¾ pound total),
    cut into thick wedges

2 nectarines (¾ pound total),
    cut into thick wedges

2 black plums (¾ pound total),
    cut into thick wedges

⅓ cup plus 3 tablespoons
    granulated sugar

2 bay leaves

1 large sprig rosemary or
    1 teaspoon dried rosemary

1½ cups ricotta cheese

1 teaspoon grated orange zest

1 teaspoon pure vanilla extract

Preheat the oven to 400°F.

In a 9 × 13-inch baking dish, toss the cherries, peaches, nectarines, and plums with ⅓ cup of the sugar, the bay leaves, and rosemary. Roast for 30 minutes, or until the fruits are tender and the sugar is syrupy. Discard the bay leaves and rosemary sprig (if using).

Meanwhile, in a food processor, puree the ricotta, orange zest, vanilla, and the remaining 3 tablespoons sugar until smooth.

Serve the fruit and pan juices warm, at room temperature, or chilled with a few spoonfuls of the ricotta.

Notes

PEACH COBBLER

*B*rent's mom's summertime go-to dessert! If you'd like to dress this up some more, sprinkle the biscuit topping with sliced almonds. If peaches aren't ripe, try nectarines. If there are blackberries or raspberries available, swap them in for the blueberries. This recipe is extremely versatile.

FILLING

1½ pounds peaches

1 cup blueberries

¼ cup granulated sugar

¼ cup packed light brown sugar

3 tablespoons cornstarch

½ teaspoon ground cinnamon

⅛ teaspoon ground allspice

⅛ teaspoon salt

BISCUIT TOPPING

1¼ cups all-purpose flour
   (spooned into cup and
   leveled off)

4 tablespoons granulated sugar

1 teaspoon baking powder

½ teaspoon baking soda

½ teaspoon salt

5 tablespoons cold unsalted
   butter, cut into bits

½ cup buttermilk

1 teaspoon pure vanilla extract

Flour for the work surface

Preheat the oven to 375°F.

To make the filling: Bring a saucepan of water to a boil. Drop the peaches, one at a time, into the pan and boil for 1 minute to blanch and loosen the skins. Peel off the skin. (If the skins don't peel off easily with a paring knife, use a swivel-bladed vegetable peeler.) Cut the peaches into ½-inch-thick wedges and transfer to a bowl along with the blueberries, granulated sugar, brown sugar, cornstarch, cinnamon, allspice, and salt. Transfer to an 8 × 8-inch baking dish or six 1-cup ramekins.

To make the biscuit topping: In a bowl, whisk together the flour, 3 tablespoons of the sugar, the baking powder, baking soda, and salt. Add 4 tablespoons of the butter and, with a pastry blender or 2 knives used scissor-fashion, cut in the butter until large pea-size bits are formed. Stir in the buttermilk and vanilla.

On a lightly floured work surface, pat the dough to a ½-inch thickness. Using a biscuit cutter or a drinking glass, cut out nine 2¼-inch rounds. Place the rounds on top of the fruit. Sprinkle the biscuits with the remaining 1 tablespoon sugar and dot with the remaining 1 tablespoon butter.

Bake for 35 minutes for an 8 × 8-inch pan and 20 minutes for the ramekins, or until the fruit is bubbling and the biscuit topping is golden brown and cooked through. Serve warm or at room temperature.

Notes

BUTTERSCOTCH PUDDING

If Brent wasn't attentive during the Sunday sermon, his mom would reach into her purse and pull out a butterscotch candy to be unwrapped quietly so as not to disturb the pious. Butterscotch candy is a combination of brown sugar and butter, and the term "scotch" derives from a verb that means to score or break the confection apart before hardening. So as not to be disappointing, we've gone ahead and added actual Scotch to our butterscotch pudding, but you can leave it out if you like. We still like eating this variation on a childhood favorite straight out of the pot, before it's even cooled!

3 tablespoons unsalted butter

¾ cup packed dark brown sugar

3 tablespoons cornstarch

2 cups milk

½ teaspoon salt

3 large egg yolks

1 tablespoon Scotch

In a medium, heavy-bottom saucepan (with a light-colored interior so you can monitor the color of the butter), melt 2 tablespoons of the butter over medium heat. Cook for 2 minutes, or until the butter gets foamy, the foam subsides, and the butter is browned in spots. Remove from the heat and whisk in the brown sugar, cornstarch, ½ cup of the milk, the salt, and egg yolks.

Whisk in the remaining 1½ cups milk, return to medium heat, and cook, whisking constantly, until the mixture comes to a boil. Reduce to a simmer and cook, whisking constantly, until the pudding thickens (it'll be thick like honey). Remove from the heat and whisk in the Scotch and the remaining 1 tablespoon butter.

Transfer the pudding to a bowl. Place a sheet of plastic wrap directly on the surface of the pudding and cool to room temperature. Refrigerate until ready to serve.

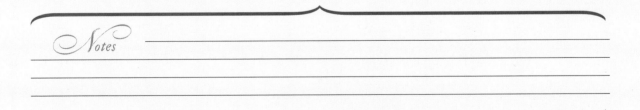

Notes

A TRIO OF ICE CREAM TOPPINGS: BLUEBERRY, CARAMEL, AND FUDGE

All of these toppings can be made ahead, stored in sterilized jars, and kept refrigerated for a few months until you're ready to use them. For the caramel and the fudge, you'll need to warm them before serving by placing the jars in a pan of warm water until the toppings have softened. Beautifully packaged, these also make great host and hostess gifts for those occasions when someone else is doing the entertaining.

BLUEBERRY TOPPING

2 cups blueberries (frozen
   berries can be used if fresh
   are not available)

3 tablespoons granulated sugar

1/4 cup water

1/4 teaspoon ground cinnamon

1/8 teaspoon ground allspice

1/8 teaspoon pepper

1 teaspoon cornstarch

1/2 teaspoon grated lemon zest

1 teaspoon fresh lemon juice

CARAMEL TOPPING

3/4 cup packed light brown sugar

1/2 cup heavy cream

3 tablespoons unsalted butter

1 teaspoon pure vanilla extract

1/4 teaspoon salt

To make the blueberry topping: In a medium saucepan, combine the blueberries, sugar, 1/4 cup water, the cinnamon, allspice, and pepper and bring to a boil over medium heat, stirring until the sugar has dissolved. Reduce to a simmer and cook for 5 minutes, or until the berries are soft and the mixture is saucy.

Meanwhile, in a small bowl, dissolve the cornstarch in 1 tablespoon cold water. Stir into the simmering blueberry mixture and cook, stirring, for 1 minute, or until thickened. Stir in the lemon zest and juice and let cool to room temperature. Serve chilled.

To make the caramel topping: In a medium saucepan, combine the brown sugar, cream, and butter and bring to a boil over medium heat. Cook, stirring frequently, for 7 to 10 minutes, or until lightly thickened. Remove from the heat and stir in the vanilla and salt. Serve warm.

To make the fudge topping: In a medium saucepan, combine the sugar, water, and corn syrup and bring to a boil over medium heat. Boil for 1 minute, then remove from the heat and stir in the cocoa powder, chocolate, and vanilla. Cover and let stand until the chocolate has melted. Serve warm.

Notes

FUDGE TOPPING

¾ cup granulated sugar

½ cup water

⅓ cup light corn syrup

¾ cup unsweetened cocoa powder

3 ounces bittersweet chocolate (60% cacao), coarsely chopped

1 teaspoon pure vanilla extract

 Notes _____

_____

_____

_____

HONEY ICE CREAM

here are 52 beehives at Beekman 1802 farm, and nothing is sweeter (literally) than the twice-a-year honey harvest. Honey comes in all different " flavors," depending on what type of flower the bees predominantly extract nectar from. If you make this ice cream with a dark honey, like buckwheat, you'll get a caramel-like ice cream; or if you choose something lighter, such as orange blossom, you'll get a light, delicate ice cream.

2 cups milk

1½ cups heavy cream

¾ cup honey

2 teaspoons grated orange zest

½ teaspoon ground cardamom

¼ teaspoon salt

1 tablespoon plus 2 teaspoons cornstarch

In a large, heavy-bottom saucepan, combine 1½ cups of the milk, the cream, honey, orange zest, cardamom, and salt and bring to a simmer.

In a small bowl, whisk the cornstarch into the remaining ½ cup milk. Add to the simmering cream mixture and cook, stirring constantly, for 1 minute, or until thickened. Let cool to room temperature.

Transfer the mixture to an ice cream machine and process according to the manufacturer's directions. Serve right away or transfer to a freezer container and freeze. If you like, serve with a drizzle of honey.

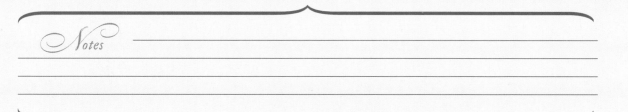

Notes

PINK GRAPEFRUIT AND CAMPARI ICE

SERVES 8

weet-tart pink grapefruit juice and bitter Campari give this ice a blush and a sophisticated flavor—a refreshing end to dinner. The alcohol keeps the juice from freezing solid, resulting in a delicious slush.

1 cup granulated sugar

2-inch piece fresh ginger, peeled and thinly sliced (about 2 tablespoons)

¾ cup water

2½ cups pink grapefruit juice

3 tablespoons Campari

In a medium saucepan, combine the sugar, ginger, and water and bring to a boil over medium heat, stirring until the sugar has dissolved. Remove from the heat and let steep for 20 minutes. Strain into a large bowl.

Stir the grapefruit juice and Campari into the ginger syrup, then transfer to an ice cream maker and process according to the manufacturer's directions. Serve right away or transfer to a freezer container and freeze.

Notes

FRUIT PIZZA
WITH SHORTBREAD COOKIE CRUST

A crisp, buttery crust, a cream cheese and sour cream topping, and a mix of summer fruit makes for a great dessert pizza. Just perfect for outdoor summer entertaining. This is a fun recipe to assemble with kids.

CRUST

8 tablespoons (1 stick) unsalted
    butter, at room temperature

1/3 cup confectioners' sugar

2 tablespoons granulated sugar

1/2 teaspoon salt

3/4 cup all-purpose flour (spooned
    into cup and leveled off)

1/4 cup cornstarch

TOPPING

6 ounces cream cheese, at room
    temperature

3 tablespoons sour cream

3 tablespoons granulated sugar

1 pound peaches and plums,
    cut into thin wedges (2 to
    2 1/2 cups)

1/4 cup seedless raspberry jam

To make the crust: Preheat the oven to 325°F.

In a food processor, combine the butter, confectioners' sugar, granulated sugar, and salt and pulse until well combined. Sprinkle the flour and cornstarch over the top and pulse until the mixture comes together. On a sheet of parchment or waxed paper, pat the dough out to a 9-inch round. Score into 8 wedges all the way through, but leave the wedges in place, and prick the dough with a fork. Bake for 25 minutes, or until golden brown and set. Let cool on the baking sheet on a wire rack.

To make the topping: Meanwhile, in a small bowl, beat together the cream cheese, sour cream, and granulated sugar until well combined.

Spread the cream cheese mixture over the cooled "pizza," leaving a 1/2-inch border all around, and top with concentric circles of peach and plum wedges.

In a small saucepan or in the microwave, melt the jam. Drizzle the jam over the fruit and cut into 8 wedges to serve.

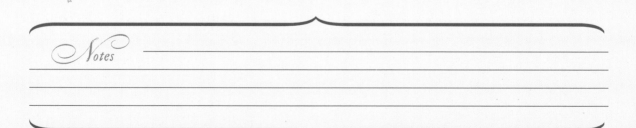

Notes

BUTTER PECAN ICE CREAM

oes butter pecan ice cream really need an introduction? The name says it all. While roasting the pecans for an hour may seem like a really long time, they'll become super-crisp and won't soften when added to the ice cream. Grade B maple syrup, which truly tastes of maple, is our choice here.

1 cup pecan halves

1 tablespoon unsalted butter, cut into bits

2 cups milk

1½ cups heavy cream

½ cup granulated sugar

¼ cup maple syrup, preferably Grade B

¼ teaspoon salt

1 tablespoon plus 2 teaspoons cornstarch

Preheat the oven to 250°F. Place the nuts on a small rimmed baking sheet and bake for 50 minutes, or until very crisp. Add the butter and bake for 10 minutes longer, or until the butter has melted. Toss to coat the nuts with the butter.

In a medium saucepan, combine the milk, 1 cup of the cream, the sugar, maple syrup, and salt and bring to a simmer. In a small bowl, stir the remaining ½ cup cream into the cornstarch, stirring until no lumps remain. Stir the cornstarch mixture into the simmering milk mixture and cook for 1 minute, stirring constantly, until lightly thickened. Remove from the heat and let cool to room temperature.

Transfer to an ice cream machine and process according to the manufacturer's directions, adding the pecans during the final couple of minutes of processing. Serve right away or transfer to a freezer container and freeze.

Notes

PEANUT BUTTER ICE CREAM

If you're a peanut lover, you'll love the taste of this. If you're a fan of those chocolate–peanut butter cups, serve it drizzled with Fudge Topping (page 179), or if you prefer the combo of peanut butter and jelly, top it with Blueberry Topping (page 178).

2 tablespoons cornstarch

1¼ cups milk

1 cup heavy cream

⅔ cup granulated sugar

1 tablespoon light corn syrup

¼ teaspoon salt

½ cup plus 1 tablespoon crunchy or creamy peanut butter

In a small bowl, whisk together the cornstarch and ½ cup of the milk. In a medium saucepan, combine the cream, sugar, corn syrup, salt, and the remaining ¾ cup milk and bring to a boil over medium heat. Whisk in the cornstarch mixture and cook, whisking constantly, for 1 minute, or until the mixture is thickened.

Remove from the heat and whisk in the peanut butter until totally melted. Let cool to room temperature, then transfer to an ice cream machine and process according to the manufacturer's directions. Serve right away or transfer to a freezer container and freeze.

Notes

SUMMER FRUIT IN WINE SYRUP

osh likes to joke that being Episcopalian meant there was never a drop of wasted wine in the house. This recipe resulted from the need to use up partial bottles of white wine and a bounty of summer fruits. If the peaches are firm, you can simply peel them with a vegetable peeler. Star anise has a flavor reminiscent of licorice and one "point" of a "star" will give this syrup a mild licorice flavor that marries well with the citrus notes of the coriander and the sweetness of the fruit. This flavor combination will also help ease the transition of the palate from summer to fall.

1 pound peaches

1 cup white wine

½ cup granulated sugar

¼ teaspoon coriander seeds

1 point of a star anise

2 cups assorted berries

Bring a small saucepan of water to a boil. Drop the peaches, one at a time, into the pan and boil for 1 minute to blanch and loosen the skins. Peel off the skin and cut the peaches into thin wedges.

In a medium saucepan, combine the wine, sugar, coriander seeds, and star anise and bring to a boil over medium heat. Boil for 3 minutes, then remove from the heat and let stand until it comes to room temperature.

In a large bowl, combine the peaches and berries. Strain the wine syrup over them and gently toss.

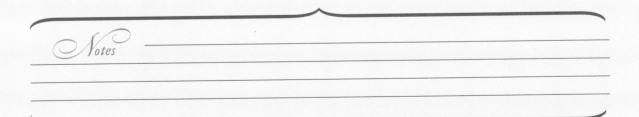

Notes

RED CURRANT JELLY CAKE

*R*ed currant jelly is a classic in European cuisines. A coating of the jelly is what gives those beautiful fruit and custard tarts that you see in pastry shops their glistening surface. Perfectly translucent red currant jelly was a culinary goal that Josh achieved soon after we started harvesting currants on the farm. Red currant jelly is not quite as sweet as some other red jams, such as raspberry or strawberry, but feel free to replace the currant jelly with either of the others. This creamy cake is perfect with a cup of coffee or tea either at dessert or for breakfast.

Softened butter for the pan

1½ cups all-purpose flour
(spooned into cup and
leveled off)

¾ cup granulated sugar

1½ teaspoons baking powder

½ teaspoon baking soda

¼ teaspoon salt

1 teaspoon ground cinnamon

10 tablespoons butter, melted

¾ cup buttermilk

1 large egg

1 large egg yolk

1 cup coarsely chopped pecans
or walnuts

¾ cup red currant jelly

Preheat the oven to 350°F. Generously butter a 9-inch cake pan.

In a large bowl, whisk together the flour, sugar, baking powder, baking soda, salt, and cinnamon.

In another bowl, whisk together the melted butter, buttermilk, whole egg, and egg yolk. Whisk in the flour mixture until just combined, then fold in the nuts. Spoon the batter into the pan and dollop the jelly over the surface. With the back of a spoon, push the jelly down into the batter.

Bake for 30 minutes, or until a wooden pick inserted in the center comes out clean with some moist crumbs attached. Let cool in the pan on a wire rack. Cut and serve from the pan.

*N*otes

BAVARIAN CREAM FRESH FRUIT TRIFLE

hen we first moved to Beekman 1802 farm, the only remnants of a once-vibrant vegetable garden was a 40-foot row of raspberries. We've since added to that with black and golden varieties—all of which come in handy in our summer menus. Here we've used raspberries and peaches, but any tender-fleshed fruit (not crisp or crunchy) will work. You'll want to prepare this in a glass bowl to show off the beautiful layers.

1 cup ricotta cheese

2 large eggs

2 large egg yolks

²⁄₃ cup granulated sugar

1 envelope (¼ ounce) plain
    unflavored gelatin

1⅓ cups milk

1 vanilla bean, split lengthwise

1 cup heavy cream

2½ cups raspberries

2 peaches (10 ounces total),
    peeled and cut into
    ½-inch wedges

3 tablespoons seedless raspberry
    jam or red currant jelly,
    melted and cooled

1 store-bought all-butter pound
    cake (about 11.5 ounces),
    cut into ½-inch-thick slices

In a food processor, whirl the ricotta until very smooth. Transfer to a large bowl.

In a medium bowl, whisk together the whole eggs, egg yolks, and sugar. In a small bowl, sprinkle the gelatin over ⅓ cup of the milk and let stand 5 minutes until swollen.

Place the remaining 1 cup milk in a medium saucepan. Scrape the vanilla seeds into the pan and add the vanilla bean. Bring to a simmer. Very slowly whisk some of the hot milk into the egg mixture to warm it, then whisk the egg mixture into the saucepan. Whisk over medium-low heat until the mixture is thick enough to coat a spoon. Whisk in the softened gelatin and stir until it has dissolved.

Place a sieve over the bowl with the ricotta in it and pour the milk mixture through the sieve into the bowl, stirring to combine. Half fill a large bowl with ice and water, and set the bowl with the ricotta mixture in it. Stir occasionally for 20 minutes, or until it starts to thicken up.

In a bowl, with an electric mixer, beat the cream until soft peaks form. Fold the whipped cream into the ricotta mixture. (This is the Bavarian cream.)

In a bowl, combine 2 cups of the raspberries, the peaches, and jam, tossing to coat. Line the bottom of a 4-quart glass bowl with slices of cake, cutting to fit. Spoon one-third of the fruit mixture over the cake and top with one-third of the Bavarian cream. Repeat to make 2 more layers. Top with the remaining ½ cup raspberries and refrigerate for 2 hours until set, or overnight.

Notes

IN-A-MINUTE MELON SORBET

here's nothing as refreshing to the tongue as a summer sorbet, and you can create this invigorating treat in mere minutes, without even breaking out the ice cream maker. The initial set-up (freezing the melon) takes more than a minute, but once that's done, this is a breeze. You can also take this mixture and freeze it in popsicle molds for a healthy summer treat that will satisfy the kids as well as the kid in you.

1 honeydew melon (about
    5 pounds), halved, seeded,
    peeled, and thinly sliced
    (8 cups)
2 tablespoons fresh lime juice
2 tablespoons honey

Spread the melon on a parchment paper-lined baking sheet and freeze until firm.

Transfer the frozen melon to a food processor along with the lime juice and honey and pulse until the consistency of sorbet. Serve immediately.

Notes _____

_____

_____

Fall

Fall

PANCAKE CAKE WITH MAPLE CREAM FROSTING *205*

OATMEAL CREAM PIES WITH GINGER CREAM *208*

ANYTHING-IN-THE-CUPBOARD NO-BAKE COOKIES *210*

INDIAN PUDDING *212* ❦ BUTTERMILK PIE WITH PECAN CRUST *213*

NEW YORK CHEESECAKE *215*

BUTTERMILK CORNBREAD PUDDING *220*

FRENCH TOAST BREAD PUDDING *221*

TARTE TATIN *223* ❦ CINNAMON BUN BUNDT CAKE *224*

STEAMED PERSIMMON PUDDING *227* ❦ HONEY-BOURBON CAKE *229*

ROASTED CARAMEL PEARS *232*

CONCORD GRAPE PIE *233* ❦ CRANBERRY-APPLE CUSTARD PIE *235*

BLACKBERRY BETTY *236* ❦ COWBOY COOKIES *239*

CHOCOLATE MAYONNAISE CAKE *240*

SOUR CREAM CUTOUT COOKIES *242*

MAPLE GRANOLA *245* ❦ PUFF PASTRY APPLE STRUDEL *247*

WALNUT CAKE (À LA GREEK DINER) *248* ❦ PUMPKIN JELLY ROLL *250*

PEAR AND QUINCE PIE *251* ❦ CARAMEL APPLES *253*

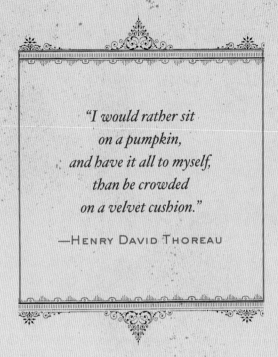

> *"I would rather sit
> on a pumpkin,
> and have it all to myself,
> than be crowded
> on a velvet cushion."*
>
> —Henry David Thoreau

After the feverish summer months, autumn brings time for a bit of reflection. Focus turns from the exterior to the interior, and the halls of the farmhouse fill with the scents of foods meant to comfort the soul. The only thing more satisfying than filling your lungs with a breath of crisp air is filling your belly with the foods that put a smile on your face.

PANCAKE CAKE WITH MAPLE CREAM FROSTING

We admit that we have had cake for breakfast before. Who hasn't? But how about breakfast for dessert? This recipe came about when we accidentally made too much pancake batter on Sunday morning. It's our take on a thousand-layer cake. The pancakes can be made up to a day ahead and refrigerated. The cake can be assembled up to 2 hours ahead. Not feeling like dessert? Prepare the pancakes using only 2 tablespoons of sugar and have them for breakfast.

PANCAKES

1 cup all-purpose flour (spooned
　　into cup and leveled off)

⅓ cup rye or whole wheat flour

2 tablespoons cornmeal

¼ cup granulated sugar

2 tablespoons light brown sugar

2 teaspoons baking powder

½ teaspoon salt

1¼ cups milk

2 large eggs

2 large egg yolks

2 tablespoons unsalted butter,
　　melted, plus more for the pan

¾ teaspoon pure vanilla extract

FILLING

11 ounces cream cheese, at room
　　temperature

¼ cup whole-milk Greek yogurt

5 tablespoons maple syrup,
　　preferably Grade B

3 tablespoons confectioners'
　　sugar, sifted

To make the pancakes: In a large bowl, whisk together the all-purpose flour, rye flour, cornmeal, granulated and brown sugars, baking powder, and salt. In a separate bowl, whisk together the milk, whole eggs, egg yolks, butter, and vanilla.

Coat an 8-inch skillet with some melted butter and heat over medium-low heat. Pour ½ cup of the batter into the pan and cook for 1½ minutes, or until large bubbles appear on the surface of the pancake. Carefully flip the pancake over and cook for 1 minute longer, or until the underside is just cooked through. Transfer to a plate and repeat with the remaining batter to make 6 pancakes and let cool to room temperature.

To make the filling: In a bowl, with an electric mixer, beat the cream cheese and yogurt until smooth. Beat in 4 tablespoons of the maple syrup and the confectioners' sugar until well combined.

To assemble the cake: Spread each pancake with one-sixth of the filling (about 5 tablespoons). Place one of the pancakes on a platter and stack the remaining pancakes on top. Drizzle the remaining 1 tablespoon maple syrup over the top of the cake.

Notes

OATMEAL CREAM PIES WITH GINGER CREAM

 atmeal cookies are Brent's favorite. These crisp, saucer-size oatmeal cookies are sandwiched with a sweet creamy filling for a takeoff on a whoopie pie.

COOKIES

1½ cups rolled oats

1 cup all-purpose flour (spooned into cup and leveled off)

¾ teaspoon baking powder

½ teaspoon baking soda

½ teaspoon ground cinnamon

¼ teaspoon freshly grated nutmeg

¼ teaspoon ground ginger

¼ teaspoon salt

8 tablespoons (1 stick) unsalted butter, at room temperature

½ cup granulated sugar

½ cup packed light brown sugar

1 large egg

FILLING

1 package (8 ounces) cream cheese, at room temperature

⅓ cup confectioners' sugar, sifted

¼ cup finely chopped crystallized ginger

TIP: *Toasting the oats beforehand not only makes them crisp but also brings out a delicious nutty flavor.*

To make the cookies: Position the racks in the upper and lower thirds of the oven and preheat to 350°F. Place the oats on a baking sheet and bake on the upper rack for 10 minutes, shaking the pan once or twice to prevent burning, until lightly browned and fragrant. Remove from the oven but leave the oven on for the cookies.

Line 2 large baking sheets with parchment or waxed paper.

In a bowl, whisk together the flour, baking powder, baking soda, cinnamon, nutmeg, ginger, and salt.

In a separate bowl, with an electric mixer on medium speed, beat the butter and the granulated and brown sugars until light and fluffy. Beat in the egg. Add the flour mixture, beating until just combined. Stir in the toasted oats.

Roll 2 tablespoons of the dough into a ball, or use a #30 ice cream scoop (1 ounce) and drop the dough 2 inches apart on the baking sheet. With dampened hands, flatten each to a ½-inch thickness.

Bake for 12 minutes, switching the baking sheets from top to bottom and rotating them from front to back halfway through, or until lightly browned around the edges and set. Let cool for 5 minutes on the baking sheets, then transfer to a wire rack to cool completely.

To make the filling: In a bowl, with an electric mixer, beat the cream cheese and confectioners' sugar until smooth. Beat in the ginger. Spread the mixture on 12 of the cookies and then top with the remaining 12 cookies.

Notes _____

_____

_____

_____

ANYTHING-IN-THE-CUPBOARD NO-BAKE COOKIES

B rent's second-favorite cookie! For years he thought his grandmother had invented these and was shocked to see how common they were. While this is our basic Beekman recipe, you can toss in any little extras from your cupboard for variation (think raisins, dates, nuts, etc.), just like Brent's grandmother used to do. These are perfect for the kids to put together.

⅓ cup packed light brown sugar

¼ cup crunchy peanut butter

1 tablespoon unsweetened cocoa powder

½ cup crunchy rice cereal

¼ cup sweetened shredded coconut

1 tablespoon milk

In a medium bowl, stir together the brown sugar, peanut butter, cocoa powder, cereal, coconut, and milk. With dampened hands, shape into 12 balls and serve.

Notes _____

INDIAN PUDDING

ndian pudding is a true heirloom recipe—one that evolved over time. Its origin is in England's hasty pudding, which was adapted by colonial Americans to be made with cornmeal instead of wheat. The pudding (really a dense cake) was sweetened with molasses when the maple syrup didn't flow so well. Tastier than it is pretty, we serve Indian pudding warm with a dollop of ice cream or whipped cream to dress it up.

Softened butter for the baking
dish

4 cups milk

⅓ cup molasses (not blackstrap)

¼ cup maple syrup, preferably
Grade B

2 tablespoons granulated sugar

3 tablespoons unsalted butter

¾ teaspoon ground ginger

½ teaspoon ground cinnamon

½ teaspoon salt

¼ teaspoon freshly grated
nutmeg

½ cup cornmeal

Preheat the oven to 300°F. Generously butter a 6-cup soufflé or baking dish.

In a medium saucepan, combine 3 cups of the milk, the molasses, maple syrup, sugar, butter, ginger, cinnamon, salt, and nutmeg and bring to a simmer over medium heat. Meanwhile, place the cornmeal in a small bowl and stir in the remaining 1 cup milk until thoroughly moistened. Whisk the cornmeal mixture into the simmering milk mixture and cook for 15 minutes, whisking frequently, or until lightly thickened.

Transfer the cornmeal mixture to the soufflé dish, smoothing the top with a knife. Bake for 2 hours, or until set and golden brown. Serve warm, topped with ice cream or whipped cream.

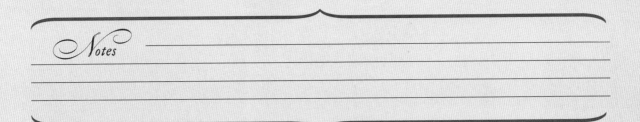

Notes

BUTTERMILK PIE WITH PECAN CRUST

his delectable pie is something Grandma might have made with pecans from the backyard tree and tangy buttermilk. This pie is sweet, rich, and just plain lovely.

CRUST

1 cup all-purpose flour (spooned into cup and leveled off)

1/3 cup pecans

3 tablespoons granulated sugar

1/2 teaspoon salt

4 tablespoons (1/2 stick) cold unsalted butter, cut into bits

1 large egg

Flour for the work surface

FILLING

1 1/4 cups granulated sugar

3 tablespoons cornstarch

3 large eggs

6 tablespoons (3/4 stick) unsalted butter, melted

1 1/3 cups buttermilk

1 teaspoon grated lemon zest

1/2 teaspoon freshly grated nutmeg

Pecans for garnish (optional)

To make the crust: In a food processor, combine the flour, pecans, sugar, and salt and pulse until the pecans are finely ground. Add the butter and egg and pulse until the dough holds together when pinched but does not form a ball. Pat into a flat disk and refrigerate for at least 30 minutes or up to a day. (Dough can be well wrapped and frozen for up to 3 months.)

On a lightly floured work surface, roll out the dough to a 12-inch round. Roll the dough around the rolling pin and then fit it into a 9-inch pie plate without stretching it, pressing the dough into the bottom and against the sides of the pan. With a pair of scissors or a paring knife, trim the dough to leave a 1-inch overhang all around. Fold the overhang in over the rim to make a double layer of dough and, with your fingers, crimp the dough around the edge. Refrigerate for at least 1 hour before baking (this helps relax the dough so it doesn't shrink when baking).

Preheat the oven to 400°F. Line the pie shell with foil or parchment paper, leaving an overhang, and fill with pie weights or dried beans to weight the crust down. Bake for 15 minutes, then remove the foil and weights and bake for 10 minutes longer or until golden. Remove the pie shell and leave the oven on but reduce the temperature to 325°F.

To make the filling: In a food processor, combine the sugar and cornstarch and pulse until combined. Add the eggs, butter, buttermilk, lemon zest, and nutmeg and process until combined.

Pour the mixture into the warm pie shell and bake for 55 minutes to 1 hour, or until the filling is set and just slightly wobbly in the center. Let cool on a wire rack. Serve at room temperature or chilled, garnished with pecans, if you like.

Notes

NEW YORK CHEESECAKE

ew York–style cheesecake was developed in the 1930s by Arnold Reuben (who also made a pretty mean sandwich). Its popularity was immediate and soon almost every New York restaurant had its own version. Of course, we had to have our own, too! Here, goat's milk yogurt gives this rich cheesecake a slight tang. If you like, you can top the cake with some berries tossed with raspberry or strawberry jam.

CRUST

Softened butter for the pan

1 cup all-purpose flour (spooned into cup and leveled off)

⅓ cup granulated sugar

1 teaspoon grated lemon zest

¼ teaspoon salt

1 large egg yolk

1 teaspoon pure vanilla extract

8 tablespoons (1 stick) cold unsalted butter, cut into bits

FILLING

1 pound cream cheese, at room temperature

1 cup granulated sugar

3 large eggs

1 large egg yolk

1½ teaspoons pure vanilla extract

1 teaspoon grated lemon zest

2 cups goat's milk yogurt

To make the crust: Preheat the oven to 350°F. Butter the bottom of a 9-inch springform pan. Line the bottom of the pan with parchment or waxed paper.

In a food processor, combine the flour, sugar, lemon zest, and salt and pulse to blend. Add the egg yolk and vanilla and pulse to combine. Add the butter and pulse until the mixture comes together when pinched between your fingers but does not form a ball. Pat the dough into the bottom and up the sides of the pan. Bake for 25 minutes, or until golden brown and cooked through. Remove from the oven and let cool to room temperature. Leave the oven on but reduce the temperature to 325°F.

To make the filling: In a food processor, combine the cream cheese and sugar and process until well blended. Add the whole eggs, egg yolk, vanilla, lemon zest, and yogurt and pulse until smooth.

Pour the filling into the crust and bake for 1 hour 15 minutes, or until firm. Let cool to room temperature, then refrigerate in the pan for 2 hours, or until completely chilled. To serve, loosen the band, release the cake, and disgard the paper.

Notes

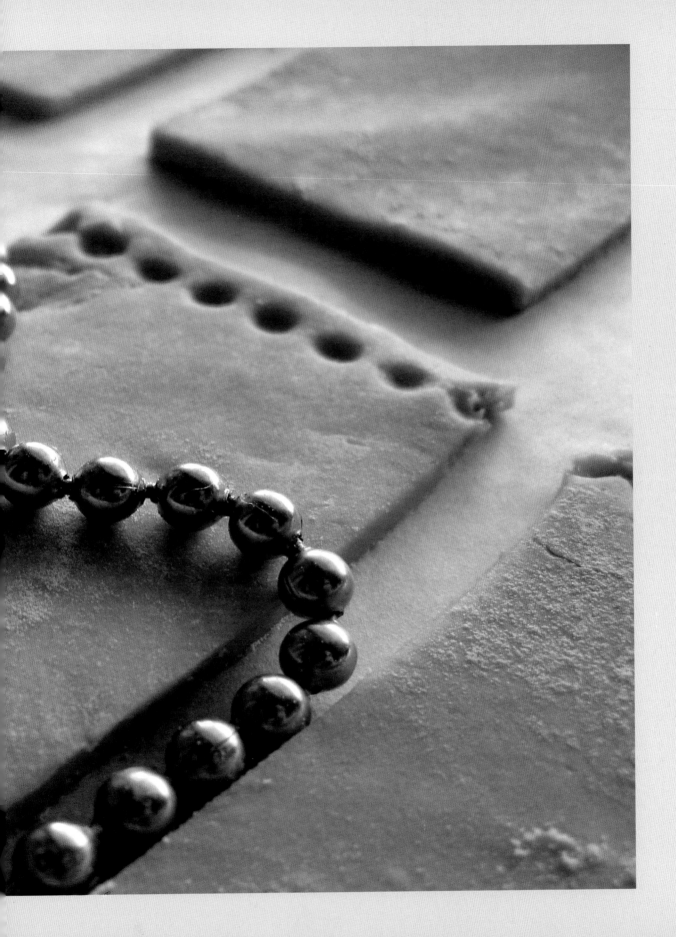

BUTTERMILK CORNBREAD PUDDING

Neither a cornbread nor a pudding, this warm, homey dessert is something often served in the South, just perfect when the first autumn chill is in the air. Serve it warm with maple syrup and puddles of heavy cream.

Softened butter for the baking
   dish

½ cup corn kernels, fresh or
   thawed frozen

¾ cup cornmeal

2 tablespoons all-purpose flour

1½ teaspoons baking powder

½ teaspoon baking soda

½ teaspoon salt

3 large eggs

4 tablespoons (½ stick) unsalted
   butter, melted

1 cup buttermilk

½ cup maple syrup, preferably
   Grade B

Maple syrup and heavy cream,
   for serving

Preheat the oven to 350°F. Butter a 9 × 9-inch baking dish.

In a food processor, pulse the corn kernels, cornmeal, flour, baking powder, baking soda, and salt until combined and the kernels have broken down somewhat. Add the eggs, butter, buttermilk, and maple syrup and process until well combined.

Pour the batter into the baking dish and bake for 35 minutes, or until set around the edges but slightly wobbly in the center and custardy.

To serve, scoop out into warm bowls and serve drizzled with maple syrup and cream.

Notes

FRENCH TOAST BREAD PUDDING

In Josh's family, Sunday mornings were time for French toast (a dish that his father somehow didn't mind making for the whole family). We've taken those flavors and made them into a dessert that's good anytime.

Softened butter for the
baking dish

3 tablespoons unsalted butter

6 ounces bread (we use
white or French, but any
can work), torn into large
pieces (6 cups)

2 tablespoons granulated sugar

½ teaspoon ground cinnamon

4 large eggs

2½ cups milk

½ cup maple syrup, preferably
Grade B

1½ teaspoons pure vanilla extract

½ teaspoon fresh grated nutmeg

Maple syrup for serving
(optional)

Butter an 8 × 8-inch baking dish.

In a large skillet, melt the unsalted butter over medium heat. Add the bread and sprinkle with 1 tablespoon of the sugar and the cinnamon. Cook, tossing frequently, for 3 to 5 minutes, or until lightly crisped and golden brown. Remove from the heat and transfer the bread to the baking dish.

In a large bowl, whisk together the eggs, milk, maple syrup, vanilla, and nutmeg. Pour the mixture over the bread and let stand for 30 minutes, or until the bread is soaked.

Preheat the oven to 350°F.

Sprinkle the top with the remaining 1 tablespoon sugar and bake for 45 minutes, or until the pudding has puffed and is set. Serve warm with additional maple syrup drizzled over the top, if desired.

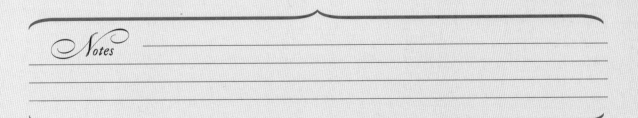

Notes

TARTE TATIN

arte Tatin—Josh's all-time favorite dessert!—is a classic French upside-down apple tart that is prepared from start to finish in just one pan. It starts with sugar that cooks in the pan until it's caramelized, and then the apples are added and cooked until they are meltingly tender. The apple filling is then topped with pastry and the pan goes into the oven. The tarte is then inverted (to the delight of everyone watching) and served. While pie dough is the typical crust used for this tart, we've swapped in store-bought puff pastry for an easier preparation.

¾ cup plus 1 tablespoon granulated sugar

2 tablespoons cider vinegar

1 vanilla bean, split lengthwise

4 tablespoons (½ stick) unsalted butter, cut into bits

2 pounds apples, peeled, cored, and quartered

1 sheet frozen all-butter puff pastry (from a 14-ounce package), thawed

TIP: *Choose a firm apple that stands up to baking without collapsing, such as Braeburn, Cortland, Golden Delicious, or a combination.*

Preheat the oven to 425°F. In a heavy-bottom 10-inch ovenproof or cast-iron skillet, stir together the ¾ cup sugar and the vinegar. Scrape the vanilla seeds into the skillet (save the vanilla bean for another use). Heat over medium heat, stirring until the sugar is thoroughly dissolved. Cook over medium heat, without stirring, for 5 minutes, or until the mixture is amber in color (like a brown paper bag). Remove from the heat. Add 2 tablespoons of the butter and the vanilla and swirl until the butter has melted. Let cool for 10 minutes.

Carefully arrange the apples over the sugar mixture in concentric circles, being careful not to touch the hot sugar mixture. Dot with the remaining 2 tablespoons butter.

Place the puff pastry over the apples and tuck the sides down around the apples. Sprinkle the 1 tablespoon sugar over the dough. Bake for 25 minutes, or until the crust is golden brown and crisp and the pan juices are bubbling. Let cool in the pan for 10 minutes, then carefully invert onto a rimmed cake plate to serve.

Notes

CINNAMON BUN BUNDT CAKE

hy not make cinnamon buns into a coffee cake that can be pulled apart when ready to serve. It's a dessert that is just meant *to make it to the breakfast table the next morning (if there's any left).*

DOUGH

1 envelope (¼ ounce, 2½ teaspoons) active dry yeast

¼ cup plus 1 teaspoon granulated sugar

¼ cup warm water (105° to 110°F)

6 tablespoons (¾ stick) unsalted butter, at room temperature

4 large egg yolks

¾ cup buttermilk

1 teaspoon salt

3½ to 4 cups all-purpose flour (spooned into cup and leveled off)

Vegetable oil for the bowl

Flour for the work surface

FILLING

4 tablespoons (½ stick) unsalted butter, melted, plus more for the pan

⅔ cup plus 3 tablespoons packed light brown sugar

1 tablespoon ground cinnamon

⅛ teaspoon salt

To make the dough: In a small bowl, dissolve the yeast and 1 teaspoon granulated sugar in the warm water. Let stand for 5 minutes, or until foamy.

Meanwhile, in a stand mixer fitted with the paddle attachment, beat the butter and ¼ cup granulated sugar until smooth. Beat in the egg yolks, buttermilk, and salt until well combined.

Beat in the yeast mixture. Beat in 3½ cups of the flour until combined. Transfer the dough to a lightly floured work surface and knead until smooth, adding more flour if necessary.

Transfer the dough to a lightly oiled bowl, cover with plastic wrap, and let stand at room temperature until doubled in volume, about 1 hour. (If you've got an 8-cup or larger clear measuring cup, use this as your bowl—this makes it really easy to see if the dough has doubled.)

To prepare the filling: Transfer the dough to a lightly floured work surface and roll to a 12 × 18-inch rectangle. Brush with 3 tablespoons of the melted butter. In a small bowl, combine the ⅔ cup brown sugar, the cinnamon, and salt and sprinkle over the dough. Starting at one short end, roll into a cylinder. Cut crosswise into 10 equal pieces.

Brush a 10- to 12-cup Bundt pan with melted butter and coat with the 3 tablespoons brown sugar. Place the pieces of dough, seam side down, around the pan, angling the pieces slightly so that no piece completely covers the swirl pattern of its neighbor. Cover with plastic wrap and let rise until light and puffed, about 45 minutes.

Preheat the oven to 350°F.

Bake for 35 minutes, or until the buns are golden brown and well risen. Remove from the oven and let cool in the pan for 5 minutes, then invert onto a cake plate. Serve warm or at room temperature.

TIP: *When purchasing packages of yeast, be sure and check the "use by" date so you are working with yeast that is truly active. If you're uncertain about the temperature of the water you're using to activate it, use an instant-read thermometer to make sure you get to 105° to 110°F.*

Notes

STEAMED PERSIMMON PUDDING

weet persimmons grow wild near Brent's childhood home, but unless you pay a visit to North Carolina to get wild persimmons, your choices in the market will be one of two types of persimmon: the round, squatty variety known as fuyu, and the elongated, egg-shaped variety known as hachiya. For this pudding you need the hachiya, which is most commonly used for baking (its pulp can even replace pumpkin in other recipes). Unripe hachiya can be very astringent, so you need them to be dead-ripe and super-soft, to the point where you think it's time to pitch them. This makes for a custardy and creamy pudding that is not overly sweet.

PUDDING

Melted butter for the pudding mold

1 cup all-purpose flour (spooned into cup and leveled off)

2 teaspoons baking soda

1 teaspoon ground cinnamon

½ teaspoon freshly grated nutmeg

½ teaspoon ground cloves

¼ teaspoon salt

2 very ripe hachiya persimmons

8 tablespoons (1 stick) unsalted butter, melted

½ cup granulated sugar

½ cup packed light brown sugar

1 large egg

1 large egg yolk

½ cup buttermilk

WHIPPED CREAM

½ cup heavy cream

3 tablespoons confectioners' sugar

½ teaspoon pure vanilla extract

To make the pudding: Get a large pot ready that is deep enough to hold a 6-cup metal pudding mold with a lid (or a 6- to 8-cup heatproof bowl). Set a wire rack or an inverted bowl in the bottom of the pan. There should also be a couple of inches of clearance at the top. Generously butter the pudding mold (or heatproof bowl).

In a medium bowl, whisk together the flour, baking soda, cinnamon, nutmeg, cloves, and salt.

Turn the persimmons stem end up and, with a spoon, scoop out the stem and discard. Scoop the flesh into a food processor and discard the skin. Puree the persimmons. Measure out 1 cup of puree and transfer to a bowl. Add the butter, granulated and brown sugars, whole egg, egg yolk, and buttermilk. Stir in the flour mixture. Pour the batter into the prepared mold. If using a pudding mold, cover with the lid; if using a bowl, cover the bowl tightly with a couple layers of foil and place a pot lid that will fit snugly on top.

Place the mold on the wire rack or inverted bowl. Pour boiling water into the pot to come halfway up the sides of the mold. Place the pot over high heat and return the water to a simmer. Reduce the heat, cover, and simmer for 1 hour 30 minutes, or until a wooden pick inserted into the pudding comes out just clean with some moist crumbs attached.

To make the whipped cream: In a medium bowl, with an electric mixer, whip the cream and confectioners' sugar until soft peaks form. Beat in the vanilla.

Invert the pudding onto a plate while still warm and serve in wedges with the whipped cream.

Notes _____

_____

_____

_____

HONEY-BOURBON CAKE

Honey cakes are often baked to usher in the Jewish New Year . . . and make it a sweet one. While lots of honey cakes are dense, this one is light and delicate, yet full-flavored.

Softened butter for the pan

Fine dried bread crumbs
    for the pan

Cooking spray

1¾ cups all-purpose flour
    (spooned into cup and
    leveled off)

1 tablespoon unsweetened
    cocoa powder

1 teaspoon ground cinnamon

½ teaspoon baking powder

½ teaspoon baking soda

½ teaspoon salt

¼ teaspoon ground cloves

½ cup vegetable oil

½ cup honey

⅓ cup brewed espresso or
    strong coffee

3 tablespoons bourbon

1 teaspoon pure vanilla extract

3 large eggs, separated

½ cup granulated sugar

⅓ cup packed dark brown sugar

Preheat the oven to 325°F. Generously butter a 10- to 12-cup Bundt pan. Dust the pan with the bread crumbs. Coat with cooking spray.

In a large bowl, whisk together the flour, cocoa powder, cinnamon, baking powder, baking soda, salt, and cloves. In a separate bowl, whisk together the oil, honey, coffee, bourbon, and vanilla.

In a bowl, with an electric mixer, beat the egg yolks and granulated and brown sugars until well combined. Add the honey mixture, beating until combined. Beat the flour in, half at a time.

In a small bowl, with an electric mixer or a whisk, beat the egg whites to stiff but not dry peaks. Spoon one-fourth of the whites into the batter and stir to lighten it a little. Gently fold in the remaining whites.

Scrape the batter into the pan and bake for 40 minutes, or until a wooden pick inserted into the center comes out clean with just a few moist crumbs attached. Let cool in the pan for 15 minutes, then run a small metal spatula around the sides and center and invert onto a wire rack to cool completely.

TIP: *Buttering the pan, dusting with crumbs, and then spraying the crumbs ensures the cake will slide out easily.*

Notes _____

_____

_____

_____

ROASTED CARAMEL PEARS

 *hile we decided not to use Bosc pears for poaching (page 156), we do like them when they're baked. Anjou pears or firm, unripe Bartletts would also work.*

3 tablespoons unsalted butter

½ cup packed light brown sugar

½ cup granulated sugar

⅛ teaspoon ground cloves

1 vanilla bean, split lengthwise

4 Bosc pears (about 6 ounces each), peeled, halved, and cored

½ teaspoon salt

5 tablespoons heavy cream

Preheat the oven to 375°F. Place the butter in an 8 × 8-inch glass baking dish and place in the oven to melt while it preheats.

Remove the baking dish from the oven and stir the brown and granulated sugars and cloves into the melted butter. Scrape in the vanilla seeds into the dish and add the vanilla bean. Place the pears, cut sides down, on the sugar mixture and sprinkle the salt over the top.

Return the dish to the oven and bake for 30 minutes, then turn the pears over and bake for 15 minutes longer, or until they can easily be pierced with a knife. (Timing will vary depending on the type of pear and how ripe they are.) Let the pears cool in the sauce.

Lift the pears out of the sauce and place on dessert plates. Remove the vanilla bean (rinse and dry it and save for another use). Transfer the sauce to a large skillet, add 3 tablespoons of the cream, and cook over medium heat for 5 minutes, or until thick enough to coat a spoon and reduced to ¾ cup. Spoon the sauce over the pears, drizzle with the remaining 2 tablespoons cream, and serve.

Notes

CONCORD GRAPE PIE

You can never have too much peanut butter and jelly, so in addition to the peanut butter crust, why not serve this intensely grape pie with a scoop of Peanut Butter Ice Cream (page 188). Concord grapes are intensely flavored and very aromatic.

CRUST

2½ cups all-purpose flour (spooned into cup and leveled off)

2 tablespoons granulated sugar

½ teaspoon salt

11 tablespoons cold unsalted butter, cut into bits

6 tablespoons creamy peanut butter

4 to 6 tablespoons ice water

Flour for the work surface

FILLING

5 cups Concord grapes (about 1½ pounds)

¾ cup granulated sugar

3 tablespoons cornstarch

1 tablespoon fresh lemon juice

¼ teaspoon ground allspice

1 tablespoon butter, cut into bits

EGG WASH

1 large egg yolk

2 tablespoons water

To make the crust: In a food processor, pulse the flour, sugar, and salt to combine. Add the butter and peanut butter and pulse until the mixture resembles coarse crumbs with some pea-size bits. Add 4 tablespoons of the ice water and pulse until the dough is crumbly but holds together when pinched, adding more ice water if needed. The dough should not come together in a ball. Divide the dough in half, wrap each half in plastic wrap, and refrigerate for 1 hour or up to 3 days.

On a lightly floured work surface, roll out one half of the dough to a 12-inch round. Roll the dough around the rolling pin and then fit it into a 9-inch pie plate without stretching it, pressing the dough into the bottom and against the sides. With a paring knife, trim the dough to leave a 1-inch overhang all around. Refrigerate for at least 1 hour before baking. Roll the other half of the dough out to a 12-inch round and refrigerate it.

To make the filling: Slip the grapes out of their skins into a saucepan, reserving the skins. Lightly mash some of the grapes and bring to a rolling boil over medium heat. Press the grape pulp through a fine-mesh sieve to remove the seeds. Transfer the puree to a bowl. Add the reserved skins, sugar, cornstarch, lemon juice, and allspice and mix well.

Preheat the oven to 400°F. Line a baking sheet with foil.

Pour the filling into the pie shell and dot it with the butter. Place the rolled-out dough on top and trim the overhang to 1 inch. Pinch the edges of the overhangs together, fold under, and crimp. Place the baking sheet on the rack below the pie to catch drips.

To make the egg wash: Beat the egg yolk with the water and brush on the pie. Make several slashes in the top for steam vents.

Bake for 40 minutes, or until the crust is golden brown and the filling is bubbling. Let cool for at least 1 hour before serving.

Notes

CRANBERRY-APPLE CUSTARD PIE

hen you think of cranberries, Thanksgiving and relish come to mind, but these tart berries also make a great pie filling or topping. Pick up a few bags when they're in season, pop them in the freezer, and you'll be able to make this pie anytime.

Basic Pie Dough (page 8)
Flour for the work surface

FILLING

3 tablespoons cornstarch

¼ cup granulated sugar

¼ cup packed light brown sugar

1 cup milk

½ cup heavy cream

2 large egg yolks

¼ teaspoon salt

1 tablespoon unsalted butter

½ teaspoon pure vanilla extract

TOPPING

2 cups fresh or frozen cranberries (no need to thaw if frozen)

2 apples (9 ounces total), peeled, cored, and cut into 1-inch chunks

¾ cup granulated sugar

To make the crust: Make the pie dough and chill as directed. On a lightly floured work surface, roll out the dough to a 12-inch round. Roll the dough around the rolling pin and then fit it into a 9-inch pie plate without stretching it, pressing the dough into the bottom and against the sides of the pan. With a pair of scissors or a paring knife, trim the dough to leave a 1-inch overhang all around. Fold the overhang in over the rim to make a double layer of dough and, with your fingers, crimp the dough around the edge. Refrigerate for at least 1 hour before baking (this helps relax the dough so it doesn't shrink when baking).

Preheat the oven to 375°F.

Line the pie shell with foil or parchment paper, leaving an overhang, and fill with pie weights or dried beans to weight the crust down. Bake for 30 minutes, then remove the foil or paper and weights and bake for 10 minutes longer, or until baked through and crisp.

To make the filling: Meanwhile, in a large, heavy-bottom saucepan, whisk together the cornstarch, granulated and brown sugars, milk, cream, egg yolks, and salt. Cook over medium-low heat whisking constantly, for 7 minutes, or until large bubbles erupt on the surface and the custard has thickened. Remove from the heat and whisk in the vanilla. Cool to room temperature.

To make the topping: Meanwhile, in a medium saucepan, combine the cranberries, apples, and sugar and bring to a boil over medium heat. Cook, stirring frequently, for 15 minutes, or until most of the cranberries have popped and the apples are tender. Let cool to room temperature. Fill the cooled pie shell with the custard and then top with the cooled cranberry-apple mixture.

Notes _____

_____

_____

_____

BLACKBERRY BETTY

*O*ur own research fails to reveal the origin of the name "Betty" to refer to a baked fruit dessert. We like to imagine she was a lovely homemaker somewhere in colonial America and that people came from far and wide to have dessert in her kitchen. We hope Betty would be thrilled with our rendition of this classic dessert, which starts with cinnamon bread and adds pepper and allspice to complement the sweet-tart flavor of the berries.

3 cups cinnamon bread cubes (¼-inch), from about 4 slices

½ cup granulated sugar

6 tablespoons (¾ stick) unsalted butter, melted

¼ teaspoon pepper

¼ teaspoon ground allspice

2 packages (6 ounces each) blackberries (about 2 cups)

1 pound apples, such as Braeburn, Cortland, or McIntosh, peeled, cored, and cut into ½-inch dice (about 2 cups)

Vanilla ice cream or whipped cream for serving (optional)

Preheat the oven to 375°F. Place the bread on a baking sheet and toast for 10 minutes, or until slightly dry. Leave the oven turned on.

Transfer the bread cubes to a bowl. Add the sugar, 4 tablespoons of the butter, the pepper, and allspice.

Brush the bottom of a 9 × 9-inch baking dish with 1 tablespoon of the butter. Scatter half of the bread mixture into the pan. Top with half of the berries and half the apples. Top with half of the remaining bread mixture, the remaining fruit, and finally the remaining bread mixture. Drizzle the 1 tablespoon butter over the top.

Cover with foil and bake for 35 minutes, or until the fruit is soft and bubbling. Serve warm or at room temperature with ice cream or whipped cream, if desired.

TIP: *Though cinnamon-raisin bread is more common, we like the simple cinnamon flavor without the raisins. Of course, if you aren't a cinnamon bread fan, you could swap in plain white bread or even brioche.*

Notes

COWBOY COOKIES

This is Josh's favorite cookie. Says Josh: "They basically combine every one of my favorite things about every other good cookie into one giant cookie heaven. They don't, however, contain real cowboys. That would be more fun than even I could handle."

1 cup all-purpose flour (spooned into cup and leveled off)

½ teaspoon salt

½ teaspoon baking powder

¼ teaspoon baking soda

8 tablespoons (1 stick) unsalted butter, at room temperature

½ cup granulated sugar

¼ cup packed light brown sugar

1 large egg

½ teaspoon pure vanilla extract

3 cups Maple Granola (page 245)

TIP: *We've used our favorite homemade granola in these chock-full-of-goodness cookies, but if you'd like, you can use your own favorite granola.*

Position the racks in the upper and lower thirds of the oven and preheat to 350°F. Line 2 large baking sheets with parchment or waxed paper.

In a medium bowl, whisk together the flour, salt, baking powder, and baking soda.

In a bowl, with an electric mixer on medium speed, beat the butter with the granulated and brown sugars until well combined. Beat in the egg and vanilla. Beat in the flour mixture. Fold in the granola.

Drop the dough by tablespoons 2 inches apart onto the baking sheets. With dampened hands, flatten the dough slightly.

Bake for 15 minutes, switching the baking sheets from top to bottom and rotating them from front to back halfway through, or until the cookies are golden around the edges and still slightly soft in the center. Let cool for 2 minutes on the pans, then transfer the cookies to a wire rack to cool completely.

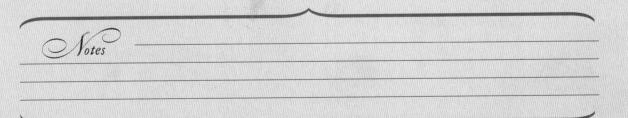

Notes

CHOCOLATE MAYONNAISE CAKE

Brent's great-grandparents raised their children amidst the Great Depression but never wanted their family to feel deprived. This cake dates back to that time period when butter was scarce. Mayo stands in for the butter or oil (and even for some of the eggs) that would typically be in a cake. If you weren't told, you'd never know that mayo was the secret ingredient.

CAKE

Softened butter for the pan

Fine dried bread crumbs for
    the pan

Cooking spray

2 cups all-purpose flour
    (spooned into cup and
    leveled off)

$1\frac{1}{4}$ teaspoons baking soda

$\frac{1}{2}$ teaspoon baking powder

$\frac{1}{4}$ teaspoon salt

$1\frac{1}{4}$ cups buttermilk

$\frac{2}{3}$ cup unsweetened cocoa
    powder

1 cup mayonnaise

2 large eggs

$\frac{3}{4}$ cup packed light brown sugar

$\frac{3}{4}$ cup granulated sugar

$1\frac{1}{2}$ teaspoons pure vanilla extract

2 ounces bittersweet chocolate
    (60% cacao), coarsely
    chopped

CHOCOLATE GLAZE

2 tablespoons honey

2 tablespoons water

$\frac{1}{4}$ cup granulated sugar

3 ounces bittersweet chocolate
    (60% cacao), coarsely
    chopped

To make the cake: Preheat the oven to 350°F. Generously butter a 10- to 12-cup Bundt pan. Dust the pan with the bread crumbs. Coat with cooking spray.

In a large bowl, whisk together the flour, baking soda, baking powder, and salt.

In a separate bowl, stir the buttermilk into the cocoa powder until thoroughly moistened. Whisk in the mayo, eggs, brown and granulated sugars, and vanilla. Fold in the flour mixture and then the chocolate.

Scrape the batter into the pan and bake for 50 to 55 minutes, or until the cake is set and a wooden pick inserted in the center comes out with some moist crumbs attached.

Let cool in the pan for 20 minutes, then run a metal spatula around the sides and center and invert the cake onto a wire rack to cool completely.

To make the chocolate glaze: In a small saucepan, combine the honey, water, and sugar over low heat until the sugar has dissolved. Remove from the heat and stir in the chocolate until smooth. Cool until no longer hot and spread over the cake.

Notes

SEE WHAT **BRENT** IS SERVING
WHEN YOU TURN THE PAGE.

SOUR CREAM CUTOUT COOKIES

andy still has the cookie cutters her mom used to make these old-time cookies: bunny rabbits, hearts, diamonds, and spades. These are mild-flavored and somehow very comforting. Sit down, get a cup of tea or coffee, and enjoy. The dough is soft, so make sure you refrigerate it for at least 2 hours before rolling.

2 cups all-purpose flour (spooned into cup and leveled off)

½ teaspoon baking soda

½ teaspoon salt

½ teaspoon freshly grated nutmeg

8 tablespoons (1 stick) unsalted butter, at room temperature

½ cup granulated sugar

¼ cup packed light brown sugar

1 large egg

1 teaspoon pure vanilla extract

⅛ teaspoon almond extract

⅓ cup sour cream

Flour for the work surface

In a bowl, whisk together the flour, baking soda, salt, and nutmeg.

In a bowl, with an electric mixer on medium speed, beat the butter and granulated and brown sugars together until smooth. Beat in the egg and vanilla and almond extracts until well combined. Add half of the flour mixture, beating only until combined. Beat in the sour cream, followed by the remaining flour mixture. Gather into a ball, divide in half, form into disks, and wrap each well in plastic wrap. Refrigerate for at least 2 hours, or until firm enough to roll out.

Preheat the oven to 400°F. Line a baking sheet (or baking sheets) with parchment or waxed paper.

On a lightly floured work surface, roll half the dough out (keep the other ball of dough refrigerated) to a ⅛- to ¼-inch thickness. Using cookie cutters, cut out shapes. Transfer to the baking sheets and bake for 9 to 11 minutes, or until golden around the edges. Let cool for 2 minutes on the baking sheets before transferring to a wire rack to cool. Repeat with the remaining dough.

Notes

MAPLE GRANOLA

Sure it's good for breakfast, but we really like using granola as a topping for ice cream—try it with the Honey Ice Cream (page 181) or the Butter Pecan Ice Cream (page 185). It is also the special ingredient in our Cowboy Cookies (page 239).

3 cups rolled oats

1½ cups nuts, such as pecans, walnuts, almonds, or hulled pumpkin seeds

½ cup maple syrup, preferably Grade B

3 tablespoons vegetable oil

¼ cup packed light brown sugar

½ teaspoon salt

Preheat the oven to 300°F.

In a large baking pan, stir together the oats and nuts. Bake for 25 to 30 minutes, or until crisp and fragrant. Increase the oven temperature to 350°F.

Meanwhile, in a small bowl, whisk together the maple syrup, oil, brown sugar, and salt.

Pour the mixture over the oats and nuts and stir to coat. Return to the oven and bake for 15 minutes, or until well set and crisp. Transfer to a large bowl to cool completely. Store in an airtight container for up to a month.

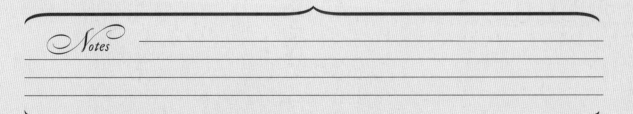

Notes

PUFF PASTRY APPLE STRUDEL

echnically, strudel should be made with strudel dough, which is like phyllo. While we like the flaky layers of phyllo pastries, we find the dough hard to work with; it dries out quickly and crumbles. Frozen puff pastry, on the other hand, is really easy to work with and makes a good substitute. When purchasing puff pastry, go for one that's made with butter.

Flour for the work surface

1 sheet frozen all-butter puff pastry (from a 14-ounce package), thawed

⅓ cup plus 1 tablespoon granulated sugar

1 teaspoon grated lemon zest

1 pound apples, such as Braeburn, peeled, quartered, cored, and thinly sliced crosswise (4 cups)

½ cup finely chopped crystallized ginger

2 tablespoons fresh lemon juice

4 tablespoons (½ stick) unsalted butter, melted

⅓ cup panko bread crumbs

Preheat the oven to 375°F. Line a rimmed baking sheet with parchment or waxed paper.

On a lightly floured work surface, roll the dough out to a 13 × 13-inch square.

In a large bowl, stir together the ⅓ cup sugar and the lemon zest. Add the apples, ginger, and lemon juice and toss to combine.

Brush the puff pastry with 3 tablespoons of the butter, scatter the bread crumbs over the butter, and top with the apple mixture, leaving a 2-inch border all around. Fold two sides in over the filling, then starting at a short end, roll the dough up jelly-roll fashion. Transfer to the baking sheet and brush with the remaining 1 tablespoon butter and sprinkle with the 1 tablespoon sugar.

Cut 4 short slashes through the top of the pastry and bake for 40 minutes, or until the top is golden brown and crisp. Let cool to room temperature before slicing.

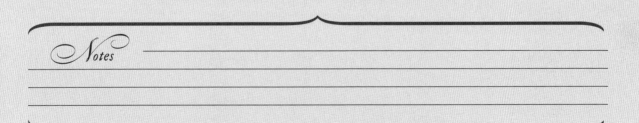

Notes

WALNUT CAKE (À LA GREEK DINER)

alnuts and bread crumbs form the structure for this cake, which gets a sugar-honey-lemon soak. It's based on some of the wonderful walnut cakes we've had at our favorite diners. Sometimes the city translates to the farm very easily.

CAKE

Softened butter for the pan

Fine dried bread crumbs for the
    pan

1¼ cups granulated sugar

5 large eggs, separated

8 tablespoons (1 stick) unsalted
    butter, melted

1½ teaspoons grated orange zest

¼ cup orange juice

2 cups walnuts, finely chopped

¾ cup fine dried bread crumbs

2 teaspoons baking powder

1 teaspoon ground cinnamon

½ teaspoon salt

¼ teaspoon ground cloves

SYRUP

½ cup granulated sugar

¼ cup honey

⅔ cup water

1 tablespoon fresh lemon juice

To make the cake: Preheat the oven to 350°F. Butter a 9-inch spring-form pan and dust with bread crumbs.

In a large bowl, whisk together the sugar, egg yolks, butter, and orange zest and juice. In a separate bowl, stir together the nuts, bread crumbs, baking powder, cinnamon, salt, and cloves. Stir the nut mixture into the sugar mixture.

In a bowl, with an electric mixer, beat the egg whites until stiff, but not dry, peaks form. Stir about one-fourth of the egg whites into the nut-sugar mixture to lighten it. Then fold the remaining whites into the bowl.

Scrape the batter into the pan and bake for 50 to 55 minutes, or until a wooden pick inserted into the center comes out clean.

To make the syrup: Meanwhile, in a heavy-bottom saucepan, combine the sugar, honey, and water. Cook over medium heat, stirring, until the sugar has dissolved. Simmer for 5 minutes to reduce slightly. Stir in the lemon juice and let cool to room temperature.

Transfer the cake, still in its pan, to a wire rack and pour the cool syrup over the hot cake. Cover with foil and let stand until cool, then release the sides of the pan.

Notes

PUMPKIN JELLY ROLL

Some things are hard to improve upon. This pumpkin roll, based on a recipe from Libby's, is a winner and so easy to do. We've upped the spices some and changed the filling just a little.

CAKE

Softened butter and flour
    for the pan

¼ cup confectioners' sugar, sifted

¾ cup all-purpose flour (spooned
    into cup and leveled off)

½ teaspoon baking powder

½ teaspoon baking soda

¾ teaspoon ground ginger

½ teaspoon ground cinnamon

¼ teaspoon ground allspice

¼ teaspoon ground cloves

¼ teaspoon freshly grated
    nutmeg

¼ teaspoon salt

3 large eggs

1 cup granulated sugar

¾ teaspoon pure vanilla extract

⅔ cup canned unsweetened
    pumpkin puree (not pumpkin
    pie filling)

FILLING

8 ounces cream cheese, at room
    temperature

⅓ cup whole-milk Greek yogurt

¾ cup confectioners' sugar,
    sifted

1 teaspoon pure vanilla extract

Confectioners' sugar for serving

To make the cake: Preheat the oven to 375°F. Butter a 10 × 15-inch jelly-roll pan. Line with parchment or waxed paper. Butter and flour the paper. Place a large kitchen towel on a work surface and dust it with the confectioners' sugar.

In a large bowl, whisk together the flour, baking powder, baking soda, ginger, cinnamon, allspice, cloves, nutmeg, and salt.

In a bowl, with an electric mixer, beat the eggs and granulated sugar until very thick. Beat in the vanilla and pumpkin puree. Beat in the flour mixture.

With a small offset spatula, evenly spread the batter in the pan. Bake for 13 to 14 minutes, or until the top springs back when lightly touched. Immediately turn the cake onto the kitchen towel. Carefully peel off the paper. Starting at one of the short ends, roll up the cake and towel together. Cool on a wire rack.

To make the filling: In a bowl, with an electric mixer, beat the cream cheese until softened. Beat in the yogurt and confectioners' sugar until smooth. Beat in the vanilla.

When the cake has cooled, unroll it and remove the towel. Spread the filling over the cake, leaving a 1-inch border all around. Starting at one short end, re-roll the cake. Dust the cake with confectioners' sugar before serving.

Notes

PEAR AND QUINCE PIE

Quince are an amazingly aromatic fruit that turn pink when cooked. But don't try eating them raw. They'll make your mouth pucker the way it would if you steeped a tea bag in your tea for too long.

Double recipe Basic Pie Dough
   (page 8)

Flour for the work surface

½ cup plus 1 tablespoon
   granulated sugar

2 tablespoons honey

1 vanilla bean, split lengthwise

2½ pounds Bosc pears, peeled
   and cut into 1-inch cubes

1 pound quince, peeled and cut
   into 1-inch cubes

2 tablespoons unsalted butter

3 tablespoons all-purpose flour

1 tablespoon heavy cream

Make the dough, divide into 2 disks, wrap, and chill as directed.

On a lightly floured work surface, roll out 1 disk of dough to a 12-inch round. Roll the dough around the rolling pin and then fit it into a 9-inch pie plate without stretching it, pressing the dough into the bottom and against the sides of the pan. With a pair of scissors or a paring knife, trim the dough to leave a 1-inch overhang all around. Refrigerate while you make the filling.

Preheat the oven to 400°F.

In a 9 × 13-inch baking pan, combine the ½ cup sugar and the honey. Scrape in the vanilla seeds, add the vanilla bean, and toss to combine. Add the pears and quince and toss again. Dot with the butter and roast for 45 minutes, or until the fruit is almost tender. Remove the vanilla bean (rinse and dry, and save it for another use). Remove from the oven and let cool to room temperature.

Stir the flour into the fruit (and its juice) mixture. Pour the fruit and its juice into the pie shell. On a lightly floured work surface, roll the second disk of dough out to a 13-inch round. Fit the dough over the pear and quince, trimming to a 1-inch overhang. Pinch the overhangs together, fold under, and with your fingers crimp and make a high fluted edge.

Brush the dough with the cream and sprinkle the 1 tablespoon sugar over the top. With a paring knife, make several slits in the top for steam vents. Bake for 35 to 45 minutes, or until the juices are bubbling and the crust is golden brown. Let cool on a wire rack before cutting.

Notes

CARAMEL APPLES

 *ou'll need a candy thermometer for these classic autumn treats. We like the contrast of the caramel coating with the salted peanuts—all against the sweet apple backdrop.*

Softened butter for the foil

4 small apples

4 long cinnamon sticks or
    lollipop sticks

1 cup granulated sugar

¼ cup maple syrup or honey

⅓ cup water

½ teaspoon salt

¼ teaspoon ground cinnamon

2 tablespoons unsalted butter

1 cup salted peanuts, coarsely
    chopped

Line a baking sheet with foil and lightly butter the foil. Poke a hole in the stem end of each apple and insert a cinnamon stick or lollipop stick.

Bring a large saucepan with a couple of inches of water to a simmer. Keep at the ready for after the caramel is made.

In a medium saucepan, combine the sugar, maple syrup, water, salt, and cinnamon and bring to a boil over medium heat, brushing the sides of the pan with a damp pastry brush to prevent any crystals from forming. Add the butter and cook the caramel, without stirring, until a candy thermometer registers 300°F.

Set the caramel pan into the larger pan of simmering water to keep the caramel warm so it won't harden. Quickly, but very carefully, dip each apple into the caramel, leaving the area around the stem uncoated. Roll the apples in the nuts to coat. Set the apples on the buttered foil to cool.

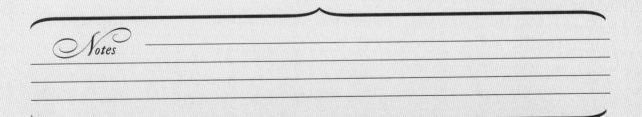

Notes

_____
_____
_____
_____
_____
_____
_____
_____
_____
_____
_____
_____
_____
_____
_____
_____
_____
_____

ACKNOWLEDGMENTS

THANK YOU TO THE ENTIRE "HEIRLOOM" TEAM THAT RE-ASSEMBLED TO PUT TOGETHER YET ANOTHER BOOK THAT IS DESTINED TO BE AN HEIRLOOM ITSELF: SANDY, PAULETTE + RICH, THOM, PAUL.

Thanks to Christofle and Yew Tree Antiques for helping us find heirlooms from generations past and future.

Thanks to the enormous team at Rodale Books who believe in our attention to the details at Beekman 1802, especially Stephen, Elissa, and Amy.

And we are especially thankful to all of those people who were told at some point in their lives to "save room for dessert"—and did!

—Brent + Josh

INDEX

Boldfaced page references indicate photographs.

*"Parting is such sweet sorrow...
especially when you can take
some dessert with you."*

—W. BEEKMAN